THE WITCHCRAFT AND FOLKLORE
OF DARTMOOR

The Witchcraft
and Folklore
of Dartmoor

RUTH E. ST. LEGER-GORDON

ILLUSTRATED

Bell Publishing Company • *New York*

ACKNOWLEDGEMENTS

I should like to express my grateful thanks to the following:

Miss Theo Brown, folklore recorder for the Devonshire Association, for permission to quote from any of her published papers; also for allowing me to use her woodcut of "The Hairy Hand".

Lady Sayer, for lending her beautiful drawing of the "Tinners' Rabbits" device.

Dr. E. P. Jowett for his prompt help in contributing five of the photographs.

The editor of *The Western Morning News* for permitting "The Moorman's Funeral" to be reproduced from an old print, the original of which was destroyed in the Plymouth blitz of 1941.

Mr. P. J. Williams, photographic manager of Messrs. Hinton Lake and Sons, Exeter, for his skilful co-operation in producing suitable prints of all the pictures.

And to Molly and Penny who typed with critical and helpful interest.

Sticklepath (Dartmoor)   RUTH E. ST. LEGER-GORDON

CONTENTS

ILLUSTRATIONS

Bibliography

English Folk Heroes by Christina Hole

Devonshire by D. St. Leger-Gordon

The Forest of Dartmoor by Hugh Breton

Dartmoor the Beloved by Beatrice Chase

Songs of the West by Baring Gould

Dartmoor by Arthur Salmon

Dartmoor Guide by William Crossing

The Western Antiquary

Haunted Waters by O'Donnell

We See Devon by Val Doone

Brunel's Tower by Eden Phillpotts

My Occult Case Book by Frank Lind

Exploration of Dartmoor by J. L. W. Page

The Golden Bough by Frazer

The White Goddess by Robert Graves

Witches by T. C. Lethbridge

Transactions of the Devonshire Association
    1959 The Black Dog in Devon by Theo Brown
    1961 Tales of a Dartmoor Village by Theo Brown
    1946 Childe's Tombe by H. P. R. Finberg
    1890 Lady Howard of Fitzford by H. L. Radford
    1882, 1892, 1934, 1956.

THE WITCHCRAFT AND FOLKLORE
OF DARTMOOR

CHAPTER ONE

Folklore

STICKLERS for truth and scientific accuracy should ignore the subject of Folklore, with its by-products Legend and Superstition. For folklore, by its very nature is composed of inaccuracies. How could it be otherwise? It is the "lore" handed down through the centuries from generation to generation, mainly from "mouth to ear", being a study of the past recorded orally by simple folk.

Anyone listening to a piece of village gossip, retailed for the third—or even second—time, only a few hours after the event, will find himself in possession of several different versions of the facts. The old parlour-game Scandal takes a sly dig at this human failing. A short factual anecdote is whispered by one player in the group to another, then to the next, and so on, until the last relates the story as he has received it. Discrepancies from the original are usually remarkable, considering the swift and direct method of communication.

Folklore is similarly engendered. It is basically composed of truth, fiction, inaccuracies, deviations, embellishment, exaggeration, addition and omission. Where memory fails, imagination fills the gap. The resultant blend is that fascinating medley that we lump together as folklore, legend, myth and superstition.

To emphasize the point I give a recent—and in this case I may say accurate—example. When compiling material for this book, I happened to read in the Folklore Notes of a 1961 journal, which we will call Source No. 1, a vague reference to a sacrifice having been performed on Dartmoor "eight or nine years ago". Wishing to find out more about this strange incident, I wrote to the recorder of the notes who constituted Source No. 2, and by her was referred to a correspondent responsible for the information, Source No. 3. From No. 3 I received the reply that no further details were available, the story having come from a friend, Source No. 4, who assumed the incident to have occurred about *fifteen to twenty* years ago. No. 4 had apparently derived the information from a newspaper report, Source No. 5. The original reporter, presumably present at the ceremony, represented Source No. 6. In making any subsequent reference, I myself become Source No. 7. Seven independent "hand-outs" in a possible twenty-five years. So is a piece of folklore born. Accurate? No, but rich in speculation capable of individualistic interpretation by each narrator. Eden Phillpotts, with his keen psychological insight was, perhaps, very near the truth when he made Crispin, one of the characters in *Brunel's Tower* remark: "But then, no two people do tell the same story quite the same way. If they tell it in the same words even, it won't be the same story; because it filters through two different minds, and minds colour words like clay colours water." This is very true, not only words, but whole incidents being repainted in the imagination.

Folklore then, is in its inception an oral tradition. In the old days, members of isolated moorland families gathered together round the fire on dark winter evenings. Education and "lettering" were virtually nil. In any case little reading would have been possible by the light of a home-made rush-dip. For the same reason, contrary to convention, no housewife could have "plied her needle" with much success by such a feeble glimmer. Possibly she turned her spinning wheel, but in the short interval between the end of the working day and early bedtime, relaxation with folded hands for the woman and long churchwarden pipe for the man seems the more probable.

It was then, as they sat round the smouldering peat fire, that the young folk listened to the tales told by father or "granfer". These were related, as remembered from their own elders, with inevitable variations and discrepancies. Indeed, with a wide-eyed, open-mouthed audience drinking in every word, it was only to be expected that the story-teller should concoct an extra spine-chilling thrill or two for good value.

"I do hope you are going to make our flesh creep," said a member of an audience to me one day when I was about to give a lecture on Dartmoor Legends. And so, I think, it has always been. Thrills were expected; thrills were handed out, accounting perhaps for the truth of another remark made to me: "Dartmoor legends are always so gloomy. Are there *no* pleasant ones?" Well, not many. Memory retains the horrific while forgetting happier, more mundane episodes. Perhaps, too, Dartmoor tales are a reflection of the character of the country itself—stern, wild, awe-inspiring, often forbidding.

"Few moors in Great Britain are as haunted as Dartmoor is reputed to be," writes O'Donnell in his book *Haunted Waters*. By an earlier author, it was described as "a wild and wond'rous region". One would expect it therefore to be a mine of "wild and wond'rous" stories. Tales there are in plenty but not all of a really original character peculiar to the district. The explanation is simple. The very solitude and isolation that encouraged superstition also formed a barrier to its survival. For centuries Dartmoor was so remote that it was known only to those who worked there; rough farmers, tin-miners, wool-jobblers, quarry-men, pack-horse drivers. Few educated people visited it, either out of interest or for recreation, until it was opened up by Macadam's two roads at the end of the eighteenth century. By the time that the pioneer folklore collectors, such as the Brays of Tavistock and Baring Gould, had got to work, the old tales and legends were dying with the people who could have recounted them.

Many were already lost; many in process of becoming so, and that applies equally today. One is told a half-tale, perhaps of a vaguely-remembered "haunting", the details of which have been forgotten. For instance, a headless coachman (one of the many) was said to drive his coach along the Plymouth-Ashburton road. I was told, not long ago: "My mother said that as a girl she and her friends used to go down to Exeter Cross to hear it go by, but they never *saw* it." One assumes that the poor coachman, having now abandoned the unequal struggle with modern traffic, has retired permanently into the shades, and his identity will never be revealed.

Again, a headless horseman used to ride the stretch of road under Ripon Tor from Hemsworthy Gate to Cold East Cross. "Or," said that informant, "it might have been a coach, I'm not sure which. But I know it was something like that." "Something like that" alone remains of this particular folk-tale. Is it perhaps the shadowy memory of some hold-up of a coach by a highwayman, who, in accordance with the best phantom tradition, later became "headless"? This peculiar propensity which afflicts so many ghosts from Ann Boleyn—who at least had justification for her uncomfortable plight—to coachmen, horsemen, black dogs, goats and pigs, is a phantom mystery for which I can find no satisfactory explanation.

With or without heads, with two legs or four, these insubstantial wraiths are rapidly disintegrating. It is largely from the older, not the younger generation that remaining fragments of superstition are still culled. Whether the modern youngster, super-educated, super-scientific and "enlightened", will, when he in turn becomes an "elder", recollect or indeed care about any of them, seems doubtful.

The natural tendency today is to think of folklore as something essentially of the past. True, like a great tree, its roots are firmly anchored there, but its branches and twigs, becoming ever more tenuous, nevertheless reach into the present, to a degree not often realized. Richard King writing at the end of the last century, declared his belief that "almost every form of superstitious observance condemned in the Penetential of Bishop Bartholomew of Exeter in the twelfth century, may be found sheltering themselves under the Dartmoor Tors". [*sic*]

I, too, have been surprised to find so many of these superstitious beliefs still alive today, seventy years later. Many of the old, now discredited, tales yet have what might be called "modern postscripts" which seem to link together the past and present centuries upon Dartmoor. To me, this "linking" is often of greater interest than some of the tales themselves, many of which are mere variations of stereotyped legends, to be found elsewhere. Wherever these modern "postscripts" occur, I give them, just as they were told to me, without comment, leaving the reader to draw his own conclusions—if any.

The inclusion of some of the well-known "chestnuts", such as "salting down feyther" at the Warren House Inn, is unavoidable in any book endeavouring to give a fairly comprehensive collection of the old moorland stories. Where possible, however, I have tried to trace and to demonstrate the growth and constant development of Dartmoor folklore, up to the present time.

Dartmoor legends, folklore and superstitions may be divided roughly into three main categories:

(1) Those that have not originated in the area but are mere variations of a type found in many other places: pixies, black dogs, and the Wish Hounds for example.

(2) What may be described as "standard spook", that is stereotyped ghost stories which have been provided with a background of local colour or into which some well-known local character has been inserted. The legends of Binjie at Cranmere Pool and Lady Howard's nightly trips to Okehampton Castle are typical of this class.

(3) Stories that have originated in the district, such as those of Childe the Hunter, the Sittaford stone circles or of Jan and the Widecombe thunderstorm.

This is, of course, no arbitrary division. There must be, and is, considerable overlapping, also, for reasons already given, inevitable variation. Upon the whole, however, most of the stories seem to fit naturally into one or other of these three categories. Some of the well-known legends, such as that of

Lady Howard, will be found, with variable details, in almost every Dartmoor guide book. Others, like the Chagford Circles story, have, as far as I know, never before been recorded, having been related to me in the traditional manner—by word of mouth.

As an introduction to a book is seldom read I would like to add here that a list of any works consulted is given in the short bibliographical list. I must emphasize, however, that for the most part, the subject matter has been gathered *orally* over a period of years. Following lectures, talks, discussions and in ordinary conversation, I have been told many tales and incidents. All were recorded in writing as soon as I reached home—"straight from the horse's mouth" in fact.

Material for the chapters on witchcraft in particular has been collected in this way. In these circumstances, it will be readily understood that names of persons and places have purposely been omitted to avoid possible distress, embarrassment or publicity. The facts, however, are authentic.

To reiterate: folklore is essentially composed of material related "live", by word of mouth. This book, to a large extent, records that tradition.

CHAPTER TWO

Pixies—Yesterday and Today

THE best-known and most popular survival in Dartmoor folk-lore today is undoubtedly the pixy. Except in name, however, the pixy is not peculiar to Dartmoor, being merely the regional variant of the Cornish "pisky" whom he most resembles, the north country "brownie", the fairy, elf, goblin, Puck, Robin Goodfellow, the Irish leprechaun, the German kobbold, and the Scandinavian troll. All were mischievous sprites, playing the same tricks and pranks upon unsuspecting mortals by whom they might sometimes be cajoled or bribed into good behaviour. With rare—and somewhat surprising—exceptions, the true Dartmoor pixy has long since vanished into the mists and mires where he properly belongs and has been successfully replaced by his commercial counterpart.

Genuine moorland folk probably ceased to believe in his existence centuries ago, the memory being kept green and fostered mainly by strangers from "up-country"—to use a local expression. These newcomers settle in moorland villages calling their renovated workmen's cottages or modern bungalows by such names as Pixy Dell, Pixy Nook, or Pixy Garden, additional versimilitude being achieved by the introduction of a gaily coloured plaster pixy sitting cross-legged upon a toadstool on the lawn. After all, if there are fairies at the bottom of the garden, why not pixies?

The cult is fostered still further by the numerous shops selling pixy-decked postcards, ashtrays, toasting forks, mugs and similar objects to tourists. Indeed, while the brownie and the leprechaun have gracefully retired to become mere fairy-tale figures, the Dartmoor pixy—possibly in company with the Lincoln Imp—has "never had it so good". He no longer, from pure mischief, lures people into bogs specially bedecked for the purpose with a waving sea of "pixy-grass"—the old Dartmoor name for the bog-cotton plant (*eriophorum*). Nowadays, even an unwary walker or rider knows rather more about botany, and rather less of the pixy and his antics. Instead, however, the irrepressible little creature, this time from purely commercial motives, decoys the traveller into the shops which reproduce his likeness in the familiar green doublet and red pointed cap *ad infinitum*.

Old tales are still told, but certainly not believed, of people having been pixy-led by deliberate malice aforethought on the part of the "little folk". In other words the travellers had lost their way, by no means as foolish or as difficult as it may seem to those who have not negotiated the moor in all kinds of weather. One or two recent tragic events are proof of this. Even in clear daylight, upon the wide featureless wastes such as the two great "blanket" bogs, north and south, sense of direction is easily lost and not so easily recovered. When obscuring cold grey mist suddenly obliterates all sight and most sound, even an experienced moorman "leaves it to the pony" he is riding to pick its own way home with reins dangling loose. In such conditions, when the mist lifts as suddenly as it descended, one may well find oneself standing on a hummock surrounded by white fluffy heads nodding as though in derision from the encircling bog into which one has blindly strayed. The expression "I was properly pixy-led" is still used jokingly round about the moor when someone has inexplicably lost his way. The Americanized word "pixylated" is never heard.

The old antidote for misadventure of this sort when pixies were obviously responsible was to turn one's cloak or coat inside out. This piece of craft presumably acted as a camouflage or disguise, the tables thus being turned upon the pixies who retired bamboozled. The spell being thus broken, everything resumed normality.

A practically identical piece of pixy-lore is attached to two Dartmoor springs. Each is named Fitz's Well, though that now lying in one of the Princetown Prison enclosures is usually corrupted into *Fice's Well*. According to tradition, in each instance a pixy-led couple, riding across the moor, abandoned the unequal struggle with their tormentors upon reaching the respective springs. Here they dismounted, turned their cloaks, watered their horses then refreshed themselves with an ice-cold draught. This produced an immediate and miraculous effect, restoring them to sanity and civilization simultaneously. In gratitude they commemorated their delivery by protecting the potent waters from defilement by a little stone canopied enclosure over Fice's Well, upon which are carved the initials I.F. with the almost indecipherable date 1568.

Fitz's Well, beside the Battle Camp road above Okehampton Park is marked by a granite cross bearing a small incised cross between the arms. Owing to the wet nature of the ground immediately around the spring, the cross periodically falls and is re-erected. For a long period this place enjoyed the reputation of being a "holy well"; later, like so many others of similar origin, degenerating into a mere "lucky" or "wishing" well. Its potency was supposed to be particularly effective on Easter Morning when youths and girls from Okehampton would trudge up the long steep hill from the town to deduce their chances of matrimony during the coming year from the state of the spring-water.

In actual fact, the origin of Fitz's two wells is somewhat different from the folklore version. John Fitz, grandfather of the notorious Lady Howard whose story is told in Chapter 5, lived at Fitzford, Tavistock, during the reign of Elizabeth I, all that now remains of his mansion being the arched gateway at the southern end of the town. Obviously he was interested in some of the first simple water schemes of the period, for it was he who marked the sites of the two widely separated springs by enclosing both and placing his initials I. (J) F. upon Fice's Well. The cross erected by him at Fitz's Well probably served a double purpose, as so many of the old moorland crosses did. Besides marking the spring, it would act also as a bond-stone and signpost, for at that period the Fitz family owned Oke-hampton Park whose boundary wall ran, as it still does today, past the well and alongside the track leading to the open moor.

John Fitz also introduced a piped water supply into his Fitzford estate and it is interesting to find that, besides being a contemporary, he was also a friend of Sir Francis Drake. Obviously the two men shared the same enthusiasm for water-undertakings, for it was Drake who engineered Plymouth's first water supply from Dartmoor. These innovations were doubtless something of a nine days wonder at the time. The effect was to promote both gentlemen from the ranks of ordin-ary citizens into figures of folklore. Whether either of them was ever pixy-led or not, both subsequently appear in "watery" legend.

The subject of "holy" or "wishing" wells is of great antiquity and interest, their hold upon popular imagination extending into the present day. To simple untaught minds, the ever-rising spring-waters appeared of miraculous origin and so possessed of similar properties. Together with venerable oaks, groves, stone circles and menhirs, natural "wells" played a significant part in the "old religion", being represented in the witches' bubbling cauldrons. Later they became Christianized into "holy wells"—the cauldron by a complicated process of transforma-tion finally emerging as the Holy Grail.

At Binsey, near Oxford, a holy well still lies just outside the little church, a flight of stone steps leading down to the still, green, debris-strewn uninviting water. A pamphlet, to be obtained inside the church, states that thousands of people annually visit the well, prayers being answered and cures effected. As a child, I was taken to drop pins—the most econ-omical form of present-day votive offering apparently—into a wishing well at Roche Abbey in Yorkshire. Widely extended are the twigs of the Tree of Folklore, and strange the workings of mass-publicity. Lately, the councils of two Devonshire resorts have been discussing the pros and cons of *building* wishing wells, into which coppers may be dropped for charity, as an additional tourist attraction. How little have the fundamentals of human nature changed throughout three thousand years! Sacred wells dedicated to the pale reflection of Tana the Moon-goddess; witches cauldrons, Sir Galahad, Glastonbury and the Holy Grail, a long line of kaleidoscopic change, ending in wishing wells as a tourist gimmick to advertise seaside resorts. Water is said to exercise a certain hypnotic effect upon the human brain. Most of us can stand for an indefinite period upon the edge of breaking waves, fascinated into immobility by the monotonous rhythm of ebb and flow. Somewhat similarly, it is said that gazing upon the small enclosed compass of water in a well at the moment of praying or wishing concentrates thought and resolution. Here we certainly have another aspect of the magic circle conception, discussed in Chapter 18.

Returning to pixy-lore, however, survivals of a genuine old-time belief linger perhaps in a few names scattered mainly around the outskirts of the moor. Pixies Parlour is a pile of tumbled boulders beside the public footpath leading from Sandypark to the Fingle Gorge and Bridge. Upon one of these great rocks rests a tired old Scotch pine, its trunk contorted into a comfortable sitting posture as though weariness had overcome the tree while waiting for the "little people" who no longer frolic around its feet.

An enormous single boulder, known as the Puggie Stone, lies beside Holy Street, that long Chagford lane leading moorwards. In this name we have an etymology indicating the pixy's affinity to Puck—the arch-pixy. Through Puck, Pucksie and Puggie we arrive eventually at the pixy. One would, however, rather have expected some connection between the devil, or at least the redoubtable King Arthur, and so huge a boulder.

The Pixies' House is a long, narrow, granite-slabbed cave penetrating the tumbled rock clitter of Sheepstor, where once the usual pin-offerings were placed "for the pixies". During the

Civil War, however, the cave was inhabited, not by pixies, but by cavalier fugitives who, to conceal their hiding-place from prying rustic eyes, doubtless encouraged a tale to ensure desired privacy on the part of the temporary owners.

Only once, in many talks with moorland folk, have I encountered anything that might be construed into a lingering bit of pixy-lore. That was some years ago in conversation with an old Dartmoor villager. Even then the word "pixy" was not mentioned by either of us. To have done so on my part would have been tantamount to insulting his intelligence, and on his part, to laying himself open to ridicule. His story was that one day, out on the peat-ties, his grandfather, cutting down into the peat, had dug up something that *looked* like a bowl, all covered with dirt. He picked it up and placed it carefully on a bank beside his lunch satchel, but when he went back to have his midday snack and rest—"Well, that bowl, he were clean gone. There wadn't no trace of 'un". The old man was not going to give himself away by mentioning pixies but he made it quite clear that he considered no *ordinary* bowl would have behaved in that fashion, staging a disappearing trick. I was unable to find out what the bowl had looked like, family tradition apparently having preserved no description of it. I could only guess that it might possibly have been a specimen of old clay pottery, dating perhaps even from the Bronze Age, which had been preserved intact in the peat until exposure to the air caused it to crumble away into dust. That is the only case of genuine pixy-belief—if such it were—that I had encountered until, oddly enough, quite recently. About that I shall have more to say later in this chapter.

It is curious, but nevertheless a fact, that in the Dartmoor country the mythical pixy is often confused with the natural will-o'-the-wisp, *ignis fatuis*. My husband, walking back over the moor one evening with a moorman, inquired whether he ever saw will-o'-the-wisps over the Dartmoor bogs. The curt negative in reply made it quite plain that the man thought he was being got at for a superstitious ignoramus. If jack-o'-lanterns were the origin of pixy-leading stories, they are seldom, if ever, seen nowadays. Hence perhaps this confusion in the local mind between the real and the fantastic.

Possibly the suspect jack-o'-lanterns may account for an old belief that "weird lights" were to be seen at night flickering on Long Ammicombe. This hill above the West Okement valley is a long wet ridge above whose peaty morasses will-o'-the-wisps might well dance at times. The lights, however, were attributed to the Devil who seems to have been as busy on Dartmoor as elsewhere. It was said that he sat up there on the ridge keeping watch to prevent the men of Okehampton and the men of Sourton from flying at each others' throats at a time when a deadly feud existed between the two towns. Why the Devil should have been as such pains to prevent strife rather than stir it up for once does not transpire.

So much for yesterday's pixies. But what about pixies today? As already remarked I have, somewhat surprisingly, met with several instances of apparently genuine belief in pixy-materialization at the present time, affording yet another example of folklore's continuance.

Until about seven years ago, I would have considered the Dartmoor pixy to be as dead as are Puck or Queen Mab in other parts of the country. Then, however, at the end of a lecture, a man in the audience told me of a moorland farm at which he had been staying, where, he averred, a bowl of milk was left out in the cow-shippens each night "for the pixies". As he was obviously not a true countryman, but of the visitor-residential type, I mentally substituted farm cats for pixies and concluded that either someone had been trying to pull his leg or that he was trying to pull mine. Frankly I disbelieved him. Yet since then I have had cause to wonder.

Upon a similar occasion in the summer of 1960, a lady got up and remarked that she was sorry to find that I obviously did not believe in pixies, because a friend of hers had *definitely seen them*. In an endeavour to overcome my suspected disbelief she readily supplied details. The friend had encountered four of them one day emerging from a bracken stack in one of the little rough field enclosures near Widecombe-in-the-Moor. All four were little men, two being somewhat taller than the others, and less pleasant looking than the smaller couple. All wore the traditional costume of red doublet, red pointed cap and long green hose. Pixy-fashions it seems remain conservative, unchanged since the days of Snow-White and the seven dwarfs. As this meeting took place in broad daylight, there was no possibility of mistake.

Afterwards, in commenting privately, but perhaps rather sceptically, to another person present, I found to my surprise that the incident was not considered unusual. My second informant mentioned a mutual Dartmoor acquaintance, who, she assured me, *often* sees pixies. So I left it at that.

Again, only a few weeks ago, I asked a man with whom I was discussing folklore, whether he had ever had any experiences with pixies or other little people, some remark of his having suggested the likelihood. He replied, quite frankly and sincerely, that he had once and once only, on his long Dartmoor rambles, seen a genuine pixy. The little man was seated upon one of the rocks of Fur Tor, far away from sound or sight of humanity. This pixy was *not* dressed traditionally, but wore ordinary clothes, and no word or sign passed between them. One moment the mannikin was plainly visible; the next there was nothing but the bare, grey granite. The man assured me—and one could not doubt his genuine and sincere belief in what he *thought* he had seen—that there was no possibility of the figure having been a boy or other small human.

His description of the pixy as being like a "little man", recalls the theory held by some people that pixies and other fairy folk were indeed human in origin. The ancient Celts of our land were a small race, and when displaced by successive Saxon and earlier alien invaders, many of them fled to the hills where they lived in woods and caves such as the Pixies House on Sheepstor. Their furtive sorties at dusk, or unexpected daylight emergences in isolated spots gave rise to a belief among the taller, more stalwart interlopers, that curious little beings inhabitated the great outdoors. As they appeared and vanished in so unaccountable a manner, it was supposed that they could only be of supernatural origin.

That is merely one theory, possibly strengthened by Professor Leaky's recent discovery of *homo habilis*, an early race of human beings, even smaller than pygmies. However conceived, the pixy, incredible as it may seem to many people, is still with us, the Widecombe neighbourhood being particularly favoured by them today. Miss Theo Brown refers to this in the Folklore Section of the 1960 *Transactions of the Devonshire Association*. She remarks that "the ability to see pixies is a gift", adding that it is possessed by two people known to her at the present time.

This is interesting. Here we have a very old belief bridging the centuries and reappearing today in a completely different stratum of society. It is not the true Dartmoor native who sees pixies now, but the settler from an altogether different walk of life. Indeed, I was asked only the other day by a Devonian born and bred and still living in one of our small moorland towns, whether I could explain the expression "pixy-laid". "I know about pixies, of course," she assured me, "but I don't know what the *laid* part means." She was genuinely surprised to hear that "laid" was simply the old Devon pronunciation of "led".

This incident is characteristic of the different types of Dartmoor dweller today. There is the "foreigner", to use a term now almost obsolete, who is nevertheless a genuine moor-lover enthusiastically assimilating all the old folklore. By contrast, the true native is rapidly forgetting not only the tales her mother taught her, but also the once familiar vernacular. The whole pixy situation is perhaps best summed up in a poem by T. P. Carrington:

> There's piskies up to Dartymoor
> And t'idden gude yu sez there b'aint.

And we'll leave it at that.

CHAPTER THREE

The Wish Hounds

As I begin this chapter on a stormy winter's evening under the shadow of Cosdon Beacon, surely all the wild huntsmen and all their wild men are careering madly over Dartmoor in the teeth of the raging gale. Doors bang, windows rattle, icy blasts swirl through the house, while outside the air is filled with moans, yells, shrieks and roars, as the wind batters the walls and lashes the trees. Truly, a night made for Dewer and his Wish Hounds accompanied by all the gibbering ghosts, phantom fiends and black dogs of the ages.

Dewer rides. The Devil rides. Odin, in his guise of storm-god sweeps by on the tempest, conducting the souls of the dead upwards from Earth on the wings of the wind. Dewer and the Devil are one and the same. He is the Christianized successor and representative of the ancient pagan nature-gods; Greek Pan echoed by the Rabbinical Seirissim, meaning "a goat"; Roman Mithras, Egyptian Osiris, Babylonian Tammuz. Call him what you will, he is still the horned god of age-old nature rites and fertility cults. Outlawed by the new religion, his attributes were bestowed by the Church upon the Christian personification of the Devil who retains the horns and hoofs of Pan.

He is a great huntsman. He hunts in France as *le Chasseur maudit*, the cursed huntsman whose passage across the sky presages disaster and death, as it did before the assassination of Henri Quatre. In Germany, sometimes he assumes the likeness of red-bearded Frederick Barbarrosa, or even that of the Emperor Charlemagne himself. Otherwise he is "Grünhut",

"Green Hat", incidentally an appellation also applied to Odin. This brings us to Robin Hood in his Lincoln green and Herne the Hunter haunting Windsor Forest, bearing the tell-tale antlers on his head. A step farther, and we find ourselves today looking up at the strange effigy of the "Green Man" with vegetation sprouting from hair, ears, eyes and nostrils as he appears on the capitals of pillars and on roof bosses in our churches. The old pagan has managed to slip inside, together with the sow and her litter, the "tinner's rabbits" and other emblems of the "old religion", to be perpetuated among the Christian symbols that surround them.

One might be tempted here to include the "horns of Moses" as they appear upon one of the corbels in Wimborne Minster, were it not for the fact that these curious features were something of a medieval tradition. They were even perpetuated on the great statue of Moses by Michelangelo whose approach to all religious subjects was, of course, that of a devout Christian. It is generally accepted that the horns' origin is due to a mistranslation in the Vulgate, the expression "rays of light" having been interpreted as "horns".

Since then, it seems, the austere old law-giver has, upon occasion, been legitimately adorned with these remarkable proturberances. As portrayed by Michelangelo, they are short and partially concealed by the prophet's thick, waving hair. On the Wimborne Moses, who wears his beard plaited into a neat pigtail, the horns sprout with something of a jaunty air, although the old stone-carver doubtless did his best to conform to ecclesiastical protocol.

Outdoors again in the North Country, the nature god and his phantom pack are known as Gabriel's Hounds, another odd blending of heathen and Christian mythology. Gabriel is a Christian archangel, but in Jewish fable he is lord of the underworld—like Dewer, the Devil.

"Wild-hunts" legends are as widespread as those of the little people. On Dartmoor, the Wish Hounds, like the pixies, have caught the popular imagination and remain firmly enshrined among the tors. Here, on wild stormy nights such as the present, they may be heard galloping over the moor cheered on by their huntsman Dewer, the Devil himself. Whoever is unlucky enough to meet the pack will die within the year and anyone trying to follow out of curiosity, will be lured to a nasty end. For the whole pack has an unpleasant habit of suddenly disappearing in full cry over the edge of the Dewer Stone, that precipitous crag at Dartmoor's southern tip, so named for this very reason. There they vanish and their unsuspecting follower with them—to the sounds of hollow laughter, deep baying of hounds, peals of thunder, blue flames and all appropriate phantom trappings. It is said, but upon what authority I am unable to state, that one morning, the imprints of a naked human foot were found on the extreme edge of the Dewer Stone. Close behind were the tracks of cloven hoofs—proof positive of the sequence of events. As one of the large black dogs also prowls round the foot of the crag, it is obviously a place to be avoided after dark.

According to one version, Dewer and his Wish Hounds hunt the souls of unbaptized babies. There is the story of a farmer who had been spending a convivial evening at one of the little alehouses and was riding home late across the moor. Suddenly, through the gathering darkness, he saw the Wish Hounds. Full of Dutch courage, he called out and asked whether they had enjoyed good sport, inquiring what they had caught. The Devil laughingly replied that he would make the farmer a present of their kill, and threw him a bundle. The man tucked it under his arm, and rode home. When he dismounted on his own doorstep he undid it. Inside was his own small child—dead.

Although I have come across no up-to-date appearances of the Wish Hounds equivalent to those of the pixies, belief in them certainly existed up to the end of the last century. It is on record that when a man's body was found on the banks of the River Yealm in the 1870s, the coroner's jury, unable to establish any cause of death, decided that he must have been "struck down by the phantom hunt". They wished to return a verdict of "death by supernatural agency" and were, with great difficulty, persuaded to substitute one of "accidental death" instead.

Twenty years later, a stableman in Okehampton declared that he had heard the Wish Hounds in full cry running across the moor above the town. He described how the horses in his care broke out into a heavy sweat and became so restless and unmanageable that he had difficulty in controlling them. Perhaps he had overlooked the fact that hounds, becoming separated from the hunting pack, will often follow a line of their own, giving tongue long after the main pack have gone on, or may be lost up there for hours before finding their way home to kennels.

Legend inevitably links the name of Wistman's Wood with that of the Wish Hounds. In some versions of the story the phantom pack sets out on its wild expeditions as dusk falls from the grotesque and ghostly little oak copse on the banks of the West Dart. Certainly there could be no more fitting kennel for Dewer's hounds than the huge grey boulders concealed among the lichen-bearded, contorted trunks.

Sometimes also known as the Yeth or Heath Hounds, the Wish pack is probably the "wisht" or eerie hounds, and Wistman's Wood may well be the "Whist" wood. Again it may be the wood of "whist" rocks, derived from the Celtic *maen*, a stone. Other more learned derivations have been suggested, but the whole place is steeped in "whistness" for on the open hillside above the oak copse runs the ancient Lych way, that ghostly Path of the Dead along which corpses were once carried for mile after rough mile to their burial in far-away Lydford churchyard.

Until revoked in the thirteenth century by Bishop Branscombe of Exeter by ecclesiastical decree, it was compulsory for interments to take place in the deceased's own parish churchyard, and nowhere else. Far out in the Forest of Dartmoor lie those once isolated holdings known as the Ancient Tenements, thirty-five in number. The whole of the forest is part of Lydford parish thus making it the largest in England. Funerals therefore, in medieval days, were obliged to cross the moor from their farms in the neighbourhood of Huccaby and Hexworthy to Lydford, a distance described by one old writer as "eight miles in fair weather, and fifteen in foul". At least eight bridgeless streams or rivers had to be negotiated, the last being the Tavy, the swiftest river in England. In winter spates this would involve a long stumble up one bank seeking a fordable spot, handling the coffin over slippery, sometimes submerged rocks and then retracing a parallel way down on the further bank to pick up the wandering track. Could a more terrible nightmare undertaking be imagined? It is described by my husband, D. St. Leger-Gordon, in this moving and evocative passage taken from his book *Devonshire*:

> Fearsome almost beyond belief must have been that journey over the desolate and sinister land, with the sphinx-like grey rocks ranged like perpetual mourners beside the trail, age-long recorders of every melancholy procession upon which their cold gaze had fallen; no sound save the raven's croak or the stumbling steps of the mourners "as silent and slow they followed the dead", and before them mile after toilsome mile of rock and mire and flood. . . . This must often have necessitated setting forth by the light of a flying winter moon, or the even more eerie and less effectual beams of storm-lanterns flashing like will-o'-the-wisps along the way. The most imaginative story-teller, from Scheherazade to Edgar Allen Poe, certainly never pictured a scene more wild and weird, and when the death-white mist crept down from the heights and wrapped the cold wide Moor in its spell of unreality and stillness, all the phantoms of Wistman's Wood must have mingled with the procession, the unearthly character of which no ghostly acquisition could accentuate.

Realization of this ordeal gives point to the old tale about "salting down feyther" at Warren Inn, which I repeat for the benefit of anyone who may not know it.

A traveller, staying overnight at the inn, was intrigued by a large chest standing in his bedroom. Out of curiosity he opened the lid, and to his horror found himself gazing down at a corpse. Thinking that he had discovered a murder, he rushed down to his host who reassured him by remarking casually: "There now, 'tis only feyther. Us zalted un down against when us can get un up along to Lydiford."

Or another tale of how, in an isolated farmhouse, "feyther" and the pig were bedded down in brine together. Having seen some of the huge granite salting-troughs in old moorland farm-houses, one can almost believe these—we hope exaggerated—yarns. They are related as comic episodes, but they had their origin in grim reality. There can be no doubt that until the good bishop's merciful dispensation permitted Forest burials to take place at Widecombe instead of Lydford, some really terrible crises must have arisen during severe winter isolation. Even this concession left hardship enough, and these arduous funeral processions continued to Widecombe until Chapels of Ease were built at Postbridge and Huccaby in 1868.

Small wonder then that Wistman's Wood, the Lych Path above it, and the scattered remains of a prehistoric village nearby are reputedly haunted. Echoes of these far-off times have been heard recently, when two visitors returning to the Two Bridges Hotel, after walking up the West Dart valley to Wist-man's Wood, reported having seen a phantom funeral procession of white-robed monks emerge from the lower end of the copse towards the river ford below, where they faded and disap-peared. These white-habited figures, presumably of the old Cistercian Order at Buckfast Abbey, must have been travelling far out of their usual course to be seen upon the Path of the Dead near Wistman's Wood.

A half-mile walk from the wood towards the Two Bridges road brings one to Crockern Tor, said to be the precise centre of Dartmoor where the four "quarters" into which it is divided meet. For that reason, this little tor was selected as the literal *seat* of that unique body of tin-legislators, the Stannary Parlia-ment. Ninety-six (twenty-four from each quarter) of its members allegedly met and sat together there in what must have been acute discomfort, upon the cold granite of its windy top. Not so long ago, upon dark nights, a mysterious horseman known as Old Crockern emanated from the abandoned tor, riding a skeleton horse whose bones could be heard rattling over the stones as he galloped by. Who he was, or what his errand nobody now knows and I cannot find that he has made any recent appearances. Perhaps he was an ardent Stannator who never missed a chilly session until they proved too much for both man and beast. Possibly he was a keen follower of the Wish Pack, or he may merely have been riding to join ghostly companions in nearby Wistman's Wood. Who knows? Little more than the rattling echo of his activities now remains, and very soon his memory, together with the bones of his skeleton mount, will lie disintegrated among the historical grey rocks of the tor from which he derives his name.

It has occurred to me that there may be a natural reason for the lively and long-continued memory of the Wild Hunt in its Dartmoor guise. Red deer frequented the district until practically exterminated by the Duke of Bedford's hounds in 1780 at the request of the upland sheep-farmers. Yet even today the occasional straggler is roused in bordering woodlands such as Springetts Plantations near Okehampton, or in the Holne and Buckland woods. As the deer became scarcer, the rare glimpse of a pair of antlers disappearing round a tor in gathering dusk accompanied by the sound of hoofs striking stone, may well have helped to perpetuate the age-old superstition of the horned huntsman's activities.

The story is told of a Belstone sheep-farmer who had been making a late round of his sheep one cold winter's evening. Returning along Taw Marsh in the dusk, he saw an unmistakable pair of horns just visible above the river bank. He took to his heels and never slacked progress until he reached Belstone where he reported the Devil to be lurking in Taw Marsh—obviously with evil intent towards the village. Feeling braver by daylight, next morning he assembled an escort of stalwarts and

The cross marking Fitz's Well above Okehampton

A moorman's funeral in 1932—an echo of the grim treks
along the ancient Lych Way

Buckland Abbey, Sir Francis Drake's old home

Marchant's Cross marks a branch of the Abbot's Way
along which Drake hunts the Wish Hounds

returned to the same spot. There they found a stag, frozen to death in the ice at the edge of the river.

That incident, even if largely fictitious, may throw light upon some of the Devil's later appearances, with or without his hounds upon Dartmoor. Indeed the same explanation might be applied also to many Wild Huntsmen legends elsewhere.

As an instance of how local folklore evolves, it is interesting to find that in obviously much later versions of the Wish Hounds legend, Sir Francis Drake is substituted for Dewer as the phantom huntsman, reputedly hunting the pack along that branch of the Abbot's Way that leads to his old home at Buckland Abbey. The cry of his hounds brings death to any dog hearing it. Nor is this the only legend that has built up round the man who became, indeed, almost a legendary figure during his lifetime.

Shortly before the Armada appeared, Drake, worried by lack of serviceable vessels, sat abstractedly whittling a stick—not upon Plymouth Hoe this time but upon Devil's Point. Looking down, he saw to his amazement, in the Sound below, a fleet of ships, into which every discarded chip as it touched the water had been transformed.

Everyone knows that by the construction of "Drake's Leat", parts of which still run beside the A386 highway from Yelverton to Roborough, Sir Francis gave Plymouth its first water supply. But this engineering work was preceded by the admiral riding down from Dartmoor into the city one day. Behind him, stretching back from his horse's heels like a comet's tail, flowed a copious stream of water which followed him into Plymouth.

Again, when he had purchased Buckland Abbey from his rival, Sir Richard Grenville, and was reconstructing it to his own requirements, Devils caused considerable trouble by carrying away building material at night. Drake promptly transformed himself into a seagull—an appropriate metamorphosis —and successfully routed the intruders in a series of savage attacks.

Upon another occasion when he had been absent on one of

c

his long voyages without word, his wife presumed him dead. As she stood at the altar with a would-be second husband, a cannon-ball crashed between them, a reminder that the sender was very much alive and aware of what was taking place, even if he were "in his hammock and a thousand miles away".

During the last war there were rumours—reminiscent of the First World War "Angels of Mons"—that Drake's Drum beating a ghostly tattoo had been heard once more on Plymouth Hoe.

Here one has a perfect example of folklore development, demonstrating how a famous historical character can become a legendary figure in the course of time. Often the real-life man is entirely lost in the fictitious, as Robin Hood, King Arthur or indeed that old fraud Uncle Tom Cobleigh. Around this latter indeterminate person—a mere name in a song—more nonsense accumulates every year as Widecombe Fair time comes round in September. Which gives rise to the searching question: where does nonsense end and folklore begin? Are the two synonymous? Or does nonsense, as exemplified by Drake's fictitious exploits, eventually become legitimate legend?

Whatever the answer, here we reach the point where the Wish Hounds, Dartmoor's version of a ubiquitous legend, overlaps into the second category of stories. For besides lacking incipient originality the legend m. y also be classed as "standard ghost" with the local additions of Drake, King Arthur and others as huntsmen.

There are indeed several other gentlemen, now become phantoms, who if not accredited to the "crack" Wish Hounds, nevertheless hunt their own smaller packs efficiently enough to cause disturbance on certain nights.

Drake hunts hounds along part of the Abbot's Way near Buckland Abbey. Across the moor on the east side he has an opposite number who has appropriated another portion of the same Way near Buckfastleigh as his hunting country. Wicked old hunting Squire Cabell died at the end of the seventeenth century, but his great black hounds may still be heard at night, baying along the old track. Whether they are accompanied by their former huntsman seems doubtful, for the squire lies buried just outside Buckfastleigh church under a slab of stone to *keep him down*. Above it, a special little stone porch has been built, presumably as an extra precaution to *keep down the slab*.

Among others of like habit, Squire Arscott leads a phantom pack through Tetcott Park. There is also the bad priest Dando whose hounds may be heard running along the banks of the Tamar on Sunday mornings. This, however, is following hounds rather too far from Dartmoor and its border.

Closer to its confines and in rather a different category are the Phantom Horsemen of Lustleigh Cleave. In 1956, according to my informant, she and a friend were riding over Hunters Tor one June afternoon when they encountered this unusual company, of about twelve mounted men accompanied by others on foot with greyhounds. All were in medieval costume, riding gaily caparisoned horses, one white mount with scarlet trappings being particularly conspicuous. Assuming that they had chanced upon some pageant or film shot, the two horsewomen cantered up closer keeping the party in view until it was hidden by a bend in a stone wall. Rounding the corner only a few seconds behind, the friends saw just a quiet, deserted landscape. The whole gay cavalcade had vanished literally without trace, for the women searched the ground carefully for over an hour, but the only visible hoof-prints in the soft ground were those of their own mounts.

It has been suggested that these phantom horsemen, who have apparently made former appearances, were the twelve knights of the famous 1240 Perambulation. This, however, is an error. That earlier riding-party was defining the bounds of Dartmoor Forest and so would certainly have been nowhere near Lustleigh Cleave. Possibly these gay ghosts were re-enacting some local bound-beating occasion or were merely out on a hunting foray.

CHAPTER FOUR

Black Dogs and Other Livestock

WICKED squires and black dogs, separately or in company, appear pretty frequently in the spectral hosts of Devon, as indeed do these Hounds of Hell in all counties and European countries. Why this particular type of standard "spook" should be so ubiquitous is difficult to say. There seems nothing necessarily connecting it with old custom or usage. The only really famous mythological dog was the Grecian monster Cerberus, guardian of the gates of Hades. Being attached to the dark realms of Pluto, presumably he was as sombre-coloured as his more modern counterparts. But while so many of these are afflicted with headlessness, Cerberus was over-endowed, being the possessor of three heads. The propensity for running to size has been inherited from him however, for many of his descendants are described as being as big as a calf, and if they possess heads at all they also invariably have enormous flaming eyes. One is reminded of the old Hans Andersen fairy tale in which the soldier seeking underground treasure finds it guarded by three huge dogs. The first had eyes as big as saucers, the second as big as a mill wheel while those of the third were as big as the Round Tower of Copenhagen.

Black dogs of formidable size and aspect allegedly haunt many lanes, gates and bridges throughout Devon. In contrast, however, to other reported manifestations—pixies and hairy hands for example—as well as to sensory experiences, genuine descriptions of black dog appearances in recent times are rare. The encounters are mainly in the past and I have only come across two modern instances. One of these is qualified by the statement: "I only describe an odd happening. I can't say whether the dog was real or not."

This particular meeting took place some years ago when a friend was taking her small daughter for a ride on their donkey. Going down a narrow lane leading to Okehampton Castle, they were startled by a very large black dog which jumped out of the hedge and stood glaring at them before disappearing unaccountably. The donkey's "home field", where is was accustomed to be turned loose at this juncture, was close by, yet neither persuasion nor force could induce it to go another step. The little party had to return home by a longer route. The friend, then living in Okehampton, was familiar with the lane and had never met the dog before, nor did she ever see it again. The sudden appearance of a black dog in this vicinity was of special significance as will be seen in the next chapter. In 1960 the B.B.C. got hold of this story and staged a rather disappointing "Black Dog" programme on television with Okehampton Castle as background, our friend as "heroine" and a black labrador retriever borrowed from Okehampton as the "hero" who, however, failed to appear on the screen.

The second modern instance of black dogs being seen is more positive in character. Writing to a local paper in 1958, a correspondent described a vivid memory of his boyhood. Accompanied by his parents and sister he was taken to a certain old house between Postbridge and Widecombe, a house by the way that still has the reputation of possessing an eerie atmosphere. There he was menaced by a pack of black hounds running loose in the courtyard. So fierce was their aspect that he was terrified of being bitten. Yet these frightening animals were invisible to his sister and parents, who probably dismissed the whole thing as a piece of vivid childish imagination.

I have heard more recent reports about this same house. A few years ago it was rented by a lady with her adult son and daughter. After the first night there, the son was so terrified— by what exactly was not stated—that he walked out, leaving his mother and sister to follow very shortly. He asserted that nothing would induce him to spend another night in the place. One wonders whether the son of the second story and the child of the first might possibly be one and the same person for whom the house held secret terrors.

There seem to be three separate categories of these spectral hounds:

(1)   Hounds proper, engaged in hunting, such as the Wish Pack and others described in the last chapter.

(2)   The lone "hound", so called not because of any special breed but merely to emphasize size and loping gait. Examples of these phantoms are the Yorkshire Barguest and the Lancashire Trash-hound who may be met with loping along lonely moors at night.

(3)   Black dogs embodying the spirit of some evil-doer such as Lady Howard or Weaver Knowles, whose penances in this form are described in a later chapter.

One Devonshire black dog patrols a beat from Copplestone Cross to Down St. Mary. As Black Dog hamlet lies in the same neighbourhood, it is fairly safe to assume that some old superstitious link connects the two, the origin being now forgotten.

Torrington has its black dog, and another haunts the road between Moretonhampstead and Postbridge, evincing an unusual partiality for dregs of beer. Rather optimistically, it is said to snuff about in the gutters outside public houses with this end in view. Even if no actual connection exists between pink elephants and black dogs, this particular specimen and Lady Howard's apparition outside the Royal Oak, Bridestowe, as described in Chapter 5, may derive from a common source.

Details of Devon's many black dogs have been collected and recorded by Miss Theo Brown in the *Transactions of the Devonshire Association*. She is also, I believe, preparing a book upon the subject, so to list all these creatures here would be merely tedious, particularly as like every other phantom hound up and down the county, they are all much of a muchness. They possess few distinguishing characteristics, their chief interest lying in their ubiquity and origin—the latter, as yet, obscure. Their sable hue and flaming eyes are obviously of satanic derivation, representing some form of evil emanation. One in particular, known vaguely as the "Black Dog of Dartmoor", in bygone days used to scare belated travellers, who were obliged to whip up their horses to escape pursuit. Conan Doyle undoubtedly had this phantom in mind when he wrote his Dartmoor tale, *The Hound of the Baskervilles*. His fog-shrouded Grimpen Mire where the fearsome creature finally met its death (most unfairly, I have always considered) is supposed to have been Fox-Tor Mire, the most dangerous bog on Dartmoor. It is situated south-east of Princetown, and the only convict to have escaped from Princetown Prison, never to be heard of again, is reputed to have been last seen trying to make his way across this treacherous tract of ground.

By way of pleasant and original contrast, a *white* spectral hound still haunts Cator Common, near Widecombe. Beyond that bare piece of information, I have been unable to find out anything more about this interesting individualist. Might he have been a lone survivor of that wonderful albino Celtic pack, hunted through Welsh folklore by the nature-god Arawn, this being yet another representation of Dewer and all other wild huntsmen? Arawn's unique and lovely hounds were distinguished by being pure white, and having red, translucent ears as well as flaming eyes. Surely a never-to-be forgotten sight if glimpsed through the dusk across the darkening hills. Perhaps the lost hound of Cator Common has faded back into the Celtic twilight and is now contentedly re-united with his pale phantom friends. If, on the other hand, he still awaits that day, it may not be too far distant.*

A year or so ago, a notice-board outside Headland Warren House beside the much frequented Grimspound road, invited the tourist to stop and sample a cream tea. A little later, a change of ownership brought about an obvious reversal of policy, intending visitors being warned by large white letters upon a blue background to BEWARE OF THE DOGS.

* See Postscript, *White Hound of Cator* p. 188.

This captivating notice has, unfortunately, now been removed. Its stark announcement in the lonely moorland setting conjured up visions of a new crop of Baskerville hounds, black dogs rampant and even—who knows?—of white dogs with red ears becoming incorporated into Dartmoor's folklore in the near future.

Dogs and sheep are very closely conected upon the Dartmoor hills, today in a purely business relationship, the most popular form of sheep-dog at present being the black and white collie type. In unbroken line, from Neolithic, or even Palaeolithic times, Dartmoor's oldest inhabitants are certainly the sheep. For thousands of years the hills have been dotted with their small grey shapes, indistinguishable at a distance from the rocks and boulders among which they wander. The blood of many a sheep must have been spilled upon the heather in sacrifice to the grim gods of the great stone circles, yet oddly enough, as far as I know, there are no tales or superstitions connected with ghostly sheep. Dozens of dogs, the occasional pony, pigs, goats, calves (black and headless), hares—but no sheep. This is curious, the inference being perhaps that with so many phantom hounds chasing around, any phantom flocks have by this time been worried out of existence. Nor do the shaggy moorland cattle—already appropriately clad in satanic livery—appear in anything other than reality unless, perhaps, they have been metamorphosed into some of these large dogs. Black hounds "as big as calves" are not, of course, unusual—which may explain a good many things.

There is, however, the lingering of a vague superstition covering all cattle and sheep that graze on the moor. In 1961 when visiting a small village, I was asked quite seriously whether I had heard of animals on the moor "not being what they seemed". In explanation, I was told of old moormen who knew from the behaviour and appearance of some particular sheep, bullock or pony that it was not a true beast but only the semblance of one. The difference was indefinable, being discernible only to a trained eye. The idea seemed to be that some elemental or malignant spirit had temporarily assumed the form of the animal in question and was grazing with the herd or flock. Should the moor-farmer become aware of one of these suspects, he must on no account treat it as a normal beast, or round it up with the rest. Misfortune would fall upon the other animals if he did so. Any round-up for inspection or shearing, therefore, would have to be postponed until the mysterious interloper had departed whence it came.

This superstition seems to be akin to the belief in were-wolves, or the change-over from witch to hare. Obviously it has the same origin as the old Celtic superstition found in Scotland, where the supernatural water-horse, or water-bull, rose from the loch to mingle with the herds grazing on the banks. Finding a distinct memory of this belief on the borders of Dartmoor, affords an interesting example of the long tentacles of superstition stretching out from a common ancestry in the remote past.

Apart from these suspect creatures which may appear in any flock or herd, the Dartmoor pony, like the sheep, makes few ghostly appearances. Only once have I heard a definite story of phantom ponies, and that quite recently from the daughter of the two people concerned.

She told me that her parents were returning from a bridge party one dark evening. They had just turned down Petticoat Lane leading into Throwleigh village from the open moor above, when they heard hooves behind them. The sound of ponies trotting about the Dartmoor villages at night is nothing unusual. This lane, however, is steep, dark and narrow, and feeling in danger of being run down they took refuge on the steps of one of the bungalows fronting the roadway. The galloping sound drew level and the couple felt the wind of the onrush, but no dark bodily shapes materialized out of the night. The phantom herd passed by and the tapping of their hooves gradually receded into the distance.

White horses, for obvious geological reasons have not left their mark on the Dartmoor hills. Postbridge, however, has the remnant of a headless white goat tradition. This creature occasionally jumps from a hedge, scaring horses and their riders in daylight, and has been seen more than once recently. One would like further information about this interesting survival, but detail is lacking. It seems possible that the apparition may be linked with the vague rumour to which I alluded in Chapter 1, of a goat having been sacrificed on Bel Tor a few years ago. Again, this may be but a revival of the memory of ancient sacrificial rites having been performed in that district "once upon a time".

The basis of blood-sacrifice is the belief that blood freshly-shed can emanate ectoplasm from which materialization may take place. Victims of ritual sacrifice as a rule had their throats cut from ear to ear, and in this, perhaps, lies the origin of the headless goat. The annual custom of ram-roasting at Holne on Midsummer Day, and at Kingsteignton at Whitsun, is a relic of these ancient blood-sacrifices connected with fertility rites and sun-worship. In Kingsteignton's case, the offering was also an obvious placation to the local river-god, as described in a later chapter.

From goats and sheep to pigs. Pigs are not *commonable* animals in the flesh but on Dartmoor their ghosts seem able to defy this prohibition with impunity. From Merripit Hill near Warren House Inn a phantom sow may sometimes be seen setting out with her litter of hungry little phantom piglets on a journey to Cator Gate near Widecombe. Here, it is rumoured in spectral circles, there lies a succulent dead horse. This is a curious story, reminiscent of the Three Crows who sat on a tree, or of Hawker's "rushing raven" and his hungry mate, plus a decided dash of nursery rhyme. For while the procession trots over the mist-enshrouded moor, the following delightful conversation takes place, for the wording of which I am indebted to Miss Theo Brown.

The little pigs squeak: "Starvin', starvin', starvin'." To which the old sow grunts encouragingly: "Dead 'oss, Cator Gate; dead 'oss, Cator Gate." They arrive for the anticipated feast too late. There is nothing left. Sadly they trek homewards, the piglets wailing disconsolately: "Skin and bones, skin and bones." To which their mother, aparently of true Devon breed philosophically replies: "Let 'un lie, let 'un lie." By this time the pathetic little party have become so thin and emaciated after their long trek that they dissovle into mist-wraiths, never getting back to their home ground. Nevertheless, there they all are, ready to set out again from Merripit Hill on the next occasion.

Tradition does not specify how many piglets there were in the litter. Knowledge of the exact number would be interesting, because a legend of a sow and her litter is also connected with the building of Braunton church. Here a sow with her six piglets make up the mystic number seven, featured in other sow and litter legends. A similar sow and her family of six also appear upon a roof boss of Sampford Courtenay church, making the mystic number seven.

The pig family might, at first glance, seem far removed from romanticism. Yet their claim is as valid as that of more eye-catching animals such as the antlered stag, or the horned and bearded goat. Wives are automatically accorded their husband's status in society. The sow therefore, ranks with the tusked boar as being among the creatures specially dedicated to the nature-mother-moon, apart from the fact that in her own right, the sow represents fertility. All animals bearing curved horns or tusks were dedicated to because representatives of, the "horned" or crescent moon. Even the horse was included in this august band, on account of its crescent-shaped hooves. Hence, in part at least, an explanation for the various white horses adorning hills in other parts of the country, where they were once the centres of pagan cults.

So the sow with her litter usually numbering either six or eight, parent and progeny combining to make the mystic numbers seven or nine, make periodical appearances in the pages of folklore. Her status is equal to that of white horses and goats, green men and tinners' rabbits, whether seen on church bosses and pew-ends, or materializing from the Dartmoor mists.

Yet the pig's ultra-respectability is seldom realized or recognized. In general it is considered rather as a semi-comic, somewhat unrefined butt and treated with tolerant derision. Most of the wicked in history, who after death have been condemned to expiate their crimes in bestial form, have become the inevitable black dogs. Not so the notorious Judge Jeffreys of evil memory in the West Country. He is seen haunting the scene of his Bloody Assizes at Lydford in the rather more original—if not quite so refined—guise of a large black pig. In popular estimation even satanically-bred hounds were aparently considered too good for the Judge's black spirit.

Among the "various" of Dartmoor's ghostly livestock one hears little of rabbits and hares, both of which were once far more plentiful on the hills than they are today. If the Wish Hounds have hunted their phantoms out of existence, tradition tells us nothing about it. It is indeed surprising that no legend survives of hares pursued by a phantom pack, for it is well known that witches constantly changed themselves into this form. There are accounts of hares being shot and wounded, and of the wound being found next day on the equivalent part of a witch's body, but no mention of any hunting having resulted in subsequent disappearance. Possibly black-hounds and witch-hares were too much "birds of a feather" or "phantoms of a kind" to fall foul of one another, on the honour among thieves principle.

One rather odd hare story emanates from Belstone where it was related by an old native only a few years ago. His father and a companion were walking home one evening, carrying a young hare that they had snared, in a net. As they were crossing Belstone Common above the Taw Valley, a loud voice from Cosdon Beacon behind them suddenly called distinctly: "Jacko! Jacko!" Immediately the little hare jumped up crying, "That's my dad calling me!" At which both men were so scared that they dropped the net, hare and all and made for home as fast as possible. Next day, returning to investigate, they found the net where they had dropped it but understandably—no hare. I am quite unable to make head or tail of this story, beyond reflection that the hare may have been a "jack", i.e. a male. Apart from that, I recount the story as it was told to me in Belstone. It is a typical fragment of handed-down folklore whose significance has, once again, obviously been lost in transmission.

This is a chapter about some of the phantom creatures that haunt Dartmoor. I have already mentioned that mystic emblem The Tinners' Rabbits. Although strictly it does not belong to the realms of fantasy, it is nevertheless puzzling to many people. The three rabbits, having three ears only between them, are arranged in the form of a rough triangle, the device being carved upon the roof bosses of several moorland churches—Tavistock, Chagford, South Tawton, Sampford Courtenay, North Bovey and Widecombe. Many of the Dartmoor churches are said to have been either built or restored by wealth derived from Dartmoor's tin trade, which flourished through the Middle Ages into the Elizabethan period.* Others, in like manner, were "founded upon wool". The three rabbits are an alchemical symbol representing the metal, tin, and quite probably do commemorate the munificence of some successful business man of the day. In the same way one finds the wool-staplers' insignia in other churches, almshouses and buildings—Blundell's School for example.

The rabbit emblem is, however, of much older import for it is yet another of the ancient fertility symbols, being once known as the Hunt of Venus. Both hares and rabbits were connected with moon worship and, like other pagan devices already mentioned, this little token of "the old religion" slipped into church unobtrusively, to be given a more respectable significance, as a reference to the Holy Trinity.

In more familiar but less recognizable form, the Tinners' Rabbits skip around us still on our Easter cards as the Easter Bunny, who nevertheless sports the long ears of a hare. Here, in direct line of descent it still represents fertility, the resurrec-

* See Postscript. *Tinners' Rabbits*, p. 189

tion and rebirth of nature in spring. To emphasize this point, Bunny is often accompanied by baskets of coloured eggs, symbols of new life, which, so we were told as children, it had mysteriously laid in defiance of all the laws of biology.

Some people read into Lewis Carroll's classic *Alice in Wonderland* more than meets most eyes. Besides the playing-card *motif*, they consider that the White Rabbit, leading Alice into a world of "faery" was based on this old belief. So witches, hares, Venus, Easter eggs, the White Rabbit and the Dartmoor Tinners all meet in a Wonderland as curious as that in which Alice herself wandered.

The Tinners' Rabbits as they appear on Widecombe church roof

CHAPTER FIVE

Lady Howard and Cranmere Binjy

SQUIRE CABELL, escaped from his confining masonry in Chapter 3, leads us into the second category of Dartmoor legends. Here the central figures are, like the hunting squires or Sir Francis Drake, real persons. Surrounded by appropriate ghost-trappings they have been pitched into some standardized legend in which they now appear larger than life.

In the last chapter I described the appearance of a black dog near Okehampton Castle as being of special significance. Black dogs, a headless horseman and coaches of rattling bones are good spook value anywhere. We find them all in good measure, gathered around this castle and the name of the reputedly wicked Lady Howard. Variations on her theme are numerous, her legendary exploits being as confused in detail as her real life story.

Lady *Mary*, central figure of the legend, was the granddaughter of Sir John Fitz of Fice's Well fame. Born at Fitzford House she has been inextricably confused in folklore with her notorious contemporary namesake, Lady *Frances* Howard, a Stuart beauty at the court of James I. She acquired four husbands, two of whom she is alleged to have poisoned. In her day poisoning had been brought to a fine art at the French court by Catherine de Medici, and Lady Howard took a leaf out of Catherine's book. She and her second husband were eventually sent to the Tower, accused of poisoning Sir Thomas Overbury. In these grim surroundings, before they were released, a daughter, Lady Anne, was born to them. This poor girl is said to have been hated by her mother, whose cruelty finally drove her from home.

For all these crimes Lady Howard now pays the penalty after death. Every night, according to one version of the tale, she assumes the shape of a large black dog, in which guise she runs beside a coach of bones driven by a headless coachman. The goal of the expedition is Okehampton Castle, its park in Lady Howard's day having been part of the Fitzford estates. Upon arrival she, still in dog-guise, plucks one blade of grass which she carries in her mouth back to her old home-site in Tavistock. When every blade of grass in the Castle grounds has been removed in this way at the rate of one per night, the penance will be completed, and the poor lady will be able to rest in peace. Judging by the amount of mowing still necessary around the ruins of Baldwin the Sheriff's stronghold, she has many more nocturnal journeys before her. As a reminder of the connection between Okehampton Castle, this lady, and the black dog, a path winding through the wood at the base of the keep is dedicated to her memory, being signposted as "Lady Howard's Walk".

This story has its variants. Sometimes the hound is of cyclopean breed, possessing one eye only in the middle of its forehead. Occasionally, like the coachman, it is headless, as are also "the sable steeds", but, fortunately, not all the members of the party suffer from this affliction simultaneously. In some versions the lady herself rides in the coach, being the only one, apparently, to keep her head throughout.

In this case the black dog runs alongside. Baring Gould adopts this version in *Songs of the West*:

> My Ladye hath a sable coach
> With horses two and four
> My Ladye hath a gaunt blood-hound
> That goeth on before.
> My Ladye's coach hath nodding plumes
> The driver hath no head.
> My Ladye is an ashen white
> As one that long is dead.

However she travels, there seems little doubt about the route

Lydford Keep, a castle of ill-repute, grim and haunted

The Nine Maidens Circle on Belstone Common

Lady Howard's Walk in Okehampton Castle grounds

that she follows, that being the line of the *old* main road from Tavistock to Okehampton across Blackdown. Any more suitable spot for meeting this ghostly party on a wild winter's night can scarcely be imagined. The worst of all weathers concentrates its forces on this bleak ridge, exposed to rain, mist, gales, blizzards and thunderstorms at all times of the year. Minus her escort she next turns up at Lydford Castle. An unexpected encounter here between two such august personages as Black Dog Lady Howard, and Black Pig Judge Jeffreys, should they chance to meet nose to nose round a corner of the keep, would be well worth witnessing.

Still as the black dog she is next seen in Bridestowe village, outside the "Royal Oak" public house, and again just below the village at a spot known as the Ghost Tree. Apparently she then picks up her coach somewhere on Maddaford Moor, travelling thence along the King Way, the old highroad that follows Dartmoor's edge to Okehampton, where the party finally arrives in style.

In spite of its conventional phantom trappings, this is an extremely interesting legend, and one that is still related locally, in traditional fashion. Only a month or so ago, I was told by a Bridestowe resident that "Lady Howard comes round the corner of the lane near the Shilstone Oak." This apparently insignificant detail opens up a wide background of folklore with its typical confusion between the Ghost Tree, the Shilstone Oak and the Royal Oak—probably one and the same tree. As I see it, the chain of events was linked as follows.

The name Shilstone, of prehistoric origin as explained in Chapter 7, denotes a spot of great antiquity, almost certainly the site of a long-vanished neolithic dolmen. Superstitious veneration was later transferred from this monument to some old oak growing nearby, its presence coinciding with the line of Lady Howard's nocturnal progressions. Thus it became known as the Ghost Tree. Meanwhile King Charles II's famous exploit in the Boscobel Oak engendered a crop of "royal" oaks all over Britain. Bridestowe's Shilston alias Ghost Tree was

D

then given another new look by being transformed into the Royal Oak upon an inn sign.

This legend is also a perfect example of the "standard" type, into which the person of Lady Howard has been introduced as central figure with a wealth of varying detail. Here we get the black dog, normal, cyclopean or headless; the coach of rattling bones, headless coachman and sable steeds all in the best phantom tradition as befits a high-born lady.

But what of the lady's true history? This is scarcely less confused and contradictory than her ghostly career, but its complications cannot be discussed here. Briefly, although appearing in legend as Lady *Frances* Howard, her real name seems to have been Mary, a detailed account of her life being given in a comprehensive paper entitled "Lady Howard of Fitzford" by Mrs. H. L. Radford, published in the *Transactions of the Devonshire Association* for 1890.

In this paper, the author establishes the fact of the four husbands, but there would appear to have been no poisonings and no sojourn in the Tower, nor any specified ill-treatment of the daughter. The Duke of Bedford, however, in his book *A Silver-plated Spoon*, tells rather a different story. He is a descendant of the daughter Lady Anne who married into the Russell family, and his set of husbands differs from those named by either Mrs. Radford or J. L. W. Page in his book *Exploration of Dartmoor and Its Antiquities*. All agree, however, that Lady Howard, whether Frances or Mary, was a forceful personality who left an impact upon her own day and generation. She started married life by an elopement at the age of fifteen and her selection of husbands culled from all three authors mentioned above include Sir Alan Percy, Thomas Darcy, the Earl of Essex, Robert Carr (favourite of James I), Sir Charles Howard and Sir Richard Grenville, grandson of the famous Sir Richard of *Revenge* fame. It seems a good selection from which one fact emerges clearly. In later life the lady preferred to be known by the name of her third husband, Sir Charles Howard, son of the Duke of Suffolk, and as the

infamous or notorious Lady Howard, wrongly identified with
"Frances", she takes her place in Dartmoor folklore (see Postscript, *Lady Howard*, p. 189).

Indicative of the conventional character of this legend, is
another of similar type to be found in Dunsland parish. It is,
however, but a faint echo of the more vivid activities of Lady
Howard. In a lane near Great Fulford House, not long ago one
of the old Squires Fulford might be encountered by night,
driving himself in a phantom coach drawn by four black headless horses. Why he should do so, or which particular member
of the family he was, nobody now is able to explain. Very
soon, perhaps, all the company of black dogs, shadowy coaches
and horses with their phantom handlers will have disintegrated
altogether into "air, thin air" and be remembered no more.

In the next story, of Binjy and Cranmere Pool, Binjy or Benjie
is the real life character who, like Lady Howard, has been
inserted as the peg upon which to hang another of these
standard legends. The vestry of Okehampton parish church
contains a memorial to Benjamin Gayer or Gear, five times
Mayor of Okehampton in the seventeenth century, this worthy
burgher being the Binjy of the legend. Whether he *was* as
worthy as might appear from the tablet, or whether like Lady
Howard he is a much maligned character it is impossible to
say. Justifiably or otherwise, Mayor Gayer was picked out and
plunged into the Cranmere Pool legend to sustain the part of
principal boy. According to this, he certainly fell from his
high estate.

As householder or "pot-boiler" in a venville parish,* he
exercised his right to run cattle and sheep on the moor, being
eventually accused of sheep-stealing. (Sheep stealing might
almost be described as an old Dartmoor custom, persisting
like the legend, into the present day.) As punishment for his
misdeeds he was banished to Cranmere by his fellow townsmen,
with orders to empty the pool with a sieve. But Mayor Binjy

* Venville parishes are those that still possess ancient common rights on
the Moor.

was a crafty soul. He got one up on his judges, by killing yet another sheep and using its skin to line the sieve. After that all was child's play. He soon emptied the pool and came strolling down into Okehampton. This time sterner measures were adopted. The culprit was hung near the scene of his crimes on Hangingstone Hill and then—somewhat oddly—sent back to Cranmere for a further punishment spell. This time he had to spin all the sand at the bottom of the pool into ropes and, as far as anyone knows, his ingenuity has found no way of circumventing that task as yet, but he is still up there engaged in his labours.

He is, however, not without company. There was a wicked farmer of Mary Tavy whose misdeeds remain unspecified, but who became so troublesome to his neighbours that it was decided to banish him to Cranmere. So heinous were his sins that the combined efforts of seven clergymen were needed to transform him into a colt. When this had been successfully accomplished a halter was slipped over his head and he was sent off in the charge of a farm lad. The boy had strict instructions to drop the halter when the pool was reached, then run for his life without looking round. Curiosity, however, got the better of him. He turned his head at the crucial moment, receiving a kick in the face that blinded him for life. But not before he had distinctly seen the colt disappearing under the waters of Cranmere in a ball of blue flame. (Does the will-o'-the-wisp perhaps play a part here again?)

There are also vague, fragmentary references to other malefactors having been forced into—quite literal—liquidation in Cranmere Pool, but all details are lost. It is quite certain, however, that on wild stormy nights, a belated visitor, stamping his postcard for the letter-box, may well hear the mournful sighs, groanings and wailings of Binjy, the Mary Tavy farmer and their companions in misfortune still toiling up there to fulfil the terms of their banishment. One might add that Binjy's efforts at pool-emptying and rope-weaving with sand would appear to have achieved some success. Today, there is usually

not enough water in that little peaty hollow—misnamed "pool"
to the disillusionment of many a tourist—to cover a rabbit, let
alone two or three stout gentlemen plus a full-sized colt. Nor is
there much—if any—sand. A walking stick, pushed into the
centre will go down to the handle in thick black peat-mud, so
possibly Binjy's wraith will soon be relieved of his labours.

The Binjy legend is of the same type as that of Lady Howard,
Mayor Benjamin Gayer having been placed in a standard background enhanced by local colour. The pool-emptying tale is
indeed very common, being found, with varying local adapta-
tions, in many places. On the Cornish moors, for instance, the
notoriously unjust magistrate Tregeagle spent many frustrating
years—during which, incidentally, his stature increased until
he became *Giant* Tregeagle—in trying to empty Dozmary Pool
with a leaking limpet shell. He was then transferred to Pad-
stow for a spell of sand rope-making. His cries and lamenta-
tions, however, became so disturbing to the neighbourhood
that he was once more moved on, this time to Land's End.
Here, in a cove, he perpetually sweeps out sand that is as
regularly piled up again by every tide.

Old Withat, so named from his tall white headgear, is another
sand-rope-weaver, who struggles with his disheartening task upon
the beach at Appledore.

In her paper, "Black Dogs of Devon", Miss Theo Brown
mentions yet another rope-making legend with a rather more
novel presentation. In this instance, it is William de Tracey,
one of the murderers of Thomas á Becket, who plies his sand-
craft on Braunton Burrows—an obvious source of inexhaust-
ible supply. As usual, success is never achieved for every time
a rope nears completion, a black dog appears, bearing in its
mouth a ball of fire with which it breaks or burns through the
cord, and the penance must begin all over again.

Plying his trade with the normal materials in place of sand,
Weaver Knowles once lived in Dean Prior—one-time parish of

the parson-poet Robert Herrick. Here through the Dean Combe Valley runs a charming stream, the Dean Burn, in a series of small cascades. Beneath one of these is a deepish basin known as Hound's Pool.

According to the tale, Weaver Knowles was so wedded to his craft, that even after death he refused to be parted from his loom. The vicar, having been begged by the harassed family to exorcize the industrious phantom, with great argument, difficulty and persuasion, finally lured it into the churchyard. Here he—rather meanly, I feel—seized a handful of the consecrated ground and flung it at the phantom weaver, causing an immediate transformation into a black dog. Commanding the animal to follow him to the Dean Burn the resourceful parson banished it into the deepest pool with orders to bale out every drop of water with a perforated nutshell that he had thoughtfully provided. Only when that task was completed might the industrious soul rest quietly. Whether the nutshell was to be manipulated with paws or teeth seems to have been left to the unfortunate creature's discretion. Small wonder that there is no perceptible dimunition of the water level in Hound's Pool today.

So Benjamin Gayer, the mayor; the unjust magistrate Tregeagle, William de Tracey the murderer, and Knowles the industrious weaver, each sustains the role of "hero" in a ubiquitous legend. Each has been placed in his own local environment, while Weaver Knowles, in the exalted company of Lady Howard, has been granted the black dog guise for additional good measure.

CHAPTER SIX

Childe the Hunter

As yet we have had no example of a legend that has originated on Dartmoor. Those in the last chapter certainly concerned local characters, but each had been woven into a stereotyped pattern common to many other places. However, the grim story of Childe the Hunter brings us to the third category of Dartmoor folklore in which we find legends—few in number—which really seem peculiar to the district. As Childe was a real person he must also be allowed a litle overlapping and a nodding acquaintance with Lady Howard and Benjamin Gayer in Category II.

This is perhaps the best known of all the Dartmoor tales. For this reason, although frequently quoted, it cannot well be omitted here. Indeed the story has been painstakingly and historically dissected by F. P. R. Finberg in the *Transactions of the Devonshire Association*, Volume 78. Anyone interested in trying to separate fact from fiction is referred to that scholarly paper, although at the end of it the folkloric mists remain undispersed.

The so-called Childe's Tomb today is a cross, standing near the celebrated and treacherous Fox-Tor Mire, a little south-east of Princetown. Writing early in the seventeenth century, Risdon describes this cross as "one of the three remarkable things to be seen on Dartmoor", the other two being Wistman's Wood and the reputed stone chairs and tables used by the old Stannators on Crockern Tor. The present cross of Childe's Tomb, erected beside the ruins of a prehistoric burial kist, originally stood upon three octagonal steps, but has twice been broken and restored. On the last occasion only a few years ago, it was smashed more or less accidentally by two young hikers climbing upon it to be photographed. Its repair this time was undertaken by the Dartmoor Preservation Association. Although always known as *Childe's Tomb*, the cross must have been set up originally rather as a memorial than marking an actual grave, if the old legend is indeed founded upon fact at all.

According to this, the rather mysterious Childe the Hunter was a rich young landowner living and owning estates at Plystock in the medieval period, probably during the reign of Edward III. By some he is called John, by others Amyas Childe, "Childe" being taken as his surname. Others again consider "Childe" to be merely the courtesy title given at that time to men of gentle birth, as in Byron's *Childe Harold* or Childe Roland who "to the dark tower came". However, that may be, it seems to be generally agreed that this young man went hunting one winter's day upon Dartmoor, finding himself towards the end of the day on the dreary wastes of Fox-Tor Mire, scene of subsequent tragedies, both real and fictitious. In this desolate spot he was overwhelmed by a sudden blinding blizzard. Realizing that he had no hope of finding his way off the moor in these conditions, and feeling himself becoming numbed by the cold, he adopted, as a last resource, the only course that seemed left to him. Drawing his hunting knife from its sheath, he killed his horse, opened its carcase, and crept inside in an endeavour to find a modicum of warmth and shelter from the bitter conditions raging all round him. Even this drastic measure failed to save his life, and he was frozen to death inside his sacrificed mount. One old account relates that Childe had previously made a will leaving his estates in Plymstock to the church where he should be buried. Another version tells us that when his body was recovered, a piece of paper was found beside it upon which Childe, having dipped his finger in his horse's blood had written these words:

> The first that brings me to my grave
> My lands of Plymstock he shall have.

Others say that these words had been traced upon one of the granite blocks of the old kistvaen beside which he lay. In yet a fourth variant, the words were supposed to have been traced in the frozen snow. The 'paper' is an obvious anachronism.

His failure to return led to search parties being sent out, not all it would seem from entirely disinterested motives. It is agreed that monks from Tavistock were first upon the scene, determined to remove the body for burial in their own abbey and thus become inheritors of the coveted estates. As with the "salting down feyther" episode, snow prevented the difficult journey for a while, and the body was temporarily entombed beneath the snow—hence the origin of the name, Childe's *Tomb*. This is the explanation I received from someone who had lived at Princetown and had heard the story in this form as it had been handed down in that district through the intervening centuries.

Once the entombment had been accomplished on that frozen waste, a monastic guard was mounted over the valuable corpse, day and night. One speculates why it, too, did not perish in the bitter cold. However, one expects to find irrelevances, illogicalities, and inconsistences in folklore, and this particular legend is full of them if one cares to dissect it. To continue the story, eventually the monks started on their homeward journey carrying the body upon a bier. Meanwhile the Plymstock monks from Childe's own parish got wind of what was happening. Rather naturally considering the dead man to be their own perquisite, they set out with the avowed intention of body-snatching, waiting in a little company by the ford over which their Tavistock brethren must cross the swollen, swirling River Tavy—swiftest river in England. But grapevine intelligence of the ambush had somehow reached the rival party. By a strategic deviation from the accepted route, they crossed the stream unperceived higher up by an improvised bridge, reaching their own abbey without molestation. Here they buried Childe the Hunter, thus, by the terms of his will, wherever "drawn up", receiving the rich legacy of his Plymstock possessions. Due to this incident, so continues this piece of folklore, the improvised bridge, later made more permanent, has since been known as *Guile* Bridge. Etymologists, however, will have none of this fantasy and attribute the building of the bridge to one of the Tavistock medieval trade *Guilds*, the name having been conveniently corrupted to fit neatly into the legend.

If there is any foundation of fact in this old story, Childe the Hunter quite obviously does *not* lie buried in his so-called tomb near Fox Tor. The cross was erected as a memorial at a later date, but it may well be that the spot where the body lay was, even then, correctly identified as a tomb of prehistoric origin.

This recalls the curious name of another dilapidated and practically unknown kistvaen. Its remains stand upon the northern slopes of Cosdon Beacon, just above a narrow path formerly used by whortleberry-pickers who passed along it in picturesque groups between South Zeal village and Belstone Tors to gather their purple harvest, not so long ago.

The little collection of tumbled granite slabs constituted a familiar landmark, which became much more conspicuous after the hill-side had been blackened by successive heath fires. For some reason it was always referred to as The Black Prince's Tomb; why, nobody knew, and one feels that here again is the survival of yet another now-forgotten fragment of folklore. Certainly not one of the whortleberry-gatherers, either present-day or of the past, would recognize those few tumbled stones as being any sort of prehistoric monument. Indeed, only a trained eye could discern their origin. Yet the traditional name has stuck, and one would greatly like to know how that obscure and unchartered Bronze Age grave came to be connected in the local mind with the Black Prince. Or whether the name is a corruption of some old, long-forgotten word of quite different meaning. However, if King Arthur's ghost can occasionally hunt the Wish Hounds, the Black Prince has an even better right to be commemorated on the hills of his own duchy. He was created the first Duke of Cornwall—his duchy to include also the lordship of Dartmoor—by his father Edward III who decreed that ever afterwards it should pass to the "first begotten son of the King". Nevertheless, this name provides a curious and puzzling connection between the past and present centuries on a Dartmoor hillside. Several links are missing here in a folklore chain that has both ends intact.

In contrast, an unbroken chain extending over much the same period links the story of Childe the Hunter with the present. For to this legend is attached one of these curious modern postscripts which I give without comment as it was told to me in Moretonhampstead about eight years ago.

Two girls were paying their first visit to Moreton at some date between the First and Second World Wars. They knew nothing of Dartmoor's history nor were they particularly interested. Nevertheless, being in the neighbourhood they decided to drive up one afternoon "just to have a look round". They made, of course, for that Mecca of all tourists, Princetown and the prison, after which they found themselves in the narrow lane leading to Fox-Tor Mire. Here they became aware of a little party of monks approaching, but as they had some vague idea of Buckfast Abbey and monks on Dartmoor, they thought little of it. As the monks drew nearer, however, the girls saw that they were carrying a bier. Realizing that it was a funeral procession coming towards them they pulled the car on to the grass verge, switched off the engine and waited for it to pass. When level with the car, the whole cortège disappeared into nothingness, both girls apparently witnessing this phenonmenon. On their return to Moreton, they recounted their strange experience, and then heard, for the first time, the legend of Childe the Hunter, and of how his body had been borne away from that spot by monks, centuries before.

On Gidleigh Common, between Creaber and Beaworthy stands the famous Scorhill Circle, many of whose tall granite stones have fallen or been purloined for building by moorland farmers. Roughly two and a half miles further on, upon the slopes of Sittaford Tor, are the two circles known as the Grey Wethers, all these monuments being more fully described in the next chapters. The two latter circles, although wearing a "new look" due to restoration, are as old as Scorhill, belonging to the same Bronze Age cult. Around these three circles as they stood in ancient times, is woven an extremely interesting legend, emanating from Chagford. It is of very definite local origin, nor have I heard of it elsewhere, or seen it recorded. It was told to me by an elderly Chagford man in whose family the story had been familiar for generations.

"Long ago," in the words of my narrator, "faithless wives and fickle maidens" were, like Binjy and others, compelled to expiate their misdeeds on the wilds of Dartmoor. The erring women had first to wash in Cranmere Pool, then come back across the moor to Scorhill Circle around which they had to run three times. Next they were driven down to the banks of the nearby Teign river where they were compelled to pass through the Tolmen—the holed stone in the river-bed. After this— probably purificatory—rite, the unfortunate sinners toiled up the long weary way to the Grey Wethers circles. Here, each woman fell on her knees before one of the standing stones, and prayed for forgiveness. To whom the prayer was addressed did not transpire, but if nothing happened she rose thankfully from her precarious position and returned home, purged of her transgressions. But should her sins be too heinous for remission, the huge stone fell slowly forward and crushed her.

"And that," added my informant with a twinkle in his eye, "is why so many of the stones was lying flat before they was set up again."

I find this particular legend extraordinarily interesting. Here, in considering the details, I feel sure we have more than the superficial, even mildly humorous, story that it appears to be on the surface. The roots of this one, it seems to me, lie very deeply buried in the past. It contains a hint of something fundamentally primeval, something perhaps as old as the very circles themselves. No one knows the purpose of these circles, which are more fully discussed later. When first erected about three thousand years ago, they may have encompassed religious ceremonies, serving also as meeting places where crude justice was meted out for infringement of tribal law. Surely a strong hint of these perpetrations has survived in this old Chagford tale.

Indeed, curiously enough, corroboration of the idea comes from as far away as ancient Mexico. Frazer, in *The Golden Bough* speaks of criminals being sacrificed to the sun-god at ancient harvest rituals. The manner of execution was to place the condemned person between two huge blocks of stone, so poised that at a given signal they fell together, crushing out the life of the condemned person.

Here we have a remarkable similarity between barbaric custom in ancient Mexico, and the same, as it survives in legend, on prehistoric Dartmoor. Frazer describes the sun-god's temples where huge stone blocks play a part in criminal executions. Thousands of miles away, and about the same number of years later, a similar story is related in a small Dartmoor town about the local stone circles which are considered by some archaeologists to have been temples erected for sun-worship. An astonishing coincidence, giving rise to much complicated reflection and speculation.

One discerns at least one detail of recent origin that has crept into the Chagford legend—the washing by the erring women in Cranmere Pool. Cranmere is many miles from Chagford where this story originated, and the Cranmere touch was probably first inserted after the pool had become a fashionable place of pilgrimage for Dartmoor walkers. It was only within the last hundred years that the well-known Perrott family of Chagford established themselves as Dartmoor guides. James Perrott was responsible for instituting the "letter-box" idea at Cranmere by placing first a bottle and then a tin inside a hole in the bank to receive visitors' reactions written on slips of paper. That, of course, was in the days when a walk to Cranmere from anywhere on the moor's perimeter was a pilgrimage and an achievement, triumphantly recorded by posting a card to some relative or friend stamped with the special die kept with the visitors' book. This custom, still observed, used to be called "Dropping a card on Binjy". Now the artillery roads make the approach by car an easy matter totally devoid of any sense of difficulties surmounted. From James Perrott's tin in the peat bank evolved the later solid letter-box and visitors' book, inaugurated and replaced when necessary originally by *The Western Morning News*, and now by the Dartmoor National Park Committee.

Cranmere's intrusion into the Chagford legend is, then, unlikely to be more than a hundred years old, affording a recent example of folklore's continuing evolution. Here, a modern addition has been slipped into and become an integral part of a tale of truly ancient origin.

The Tolmen (from the Celtic *tol*, hole, and *maen*, a stone) figuring in the story, is a huge boulder lying in the bed of the North Teign and containing a large natural cavity. This, formed by the river's friction, is completely perforated through into an aperture of such size that a reasonably proportioned adult clambering up on to the top of the boulder, can drop straight through to land on a conveniently placed slab of rock beneath. Of course, when the river is full and swift-flowing the feat is impossible, but normally it is easily accomplished. According to modern superstition a drop and safe landing through the Tolmen confers immunity from all rheumatic complaints. The credulous rheumatic, however, will be wise to note the height of the river before taking the plunge, otherwise his complaint will be accentuated rather than cured.

Commenting upon this superstition in a recent lecture, I jokingly remarked that I had been through the "holed-stone" several times and that, to date, I could say I was free from rheumatism. At the end of the meeting two young women came up and asked whether I would give them specific directions for finding the Tolmen. "Because," said the spokeswoman, "my friend here has very bad rheumatism and she'd like to see whether it would cure her." I was considerably non-plussed, but as they were strangers to Dartmoor I did my best to dissuade them by exaggerating the difficulties of finding the exact spot without local guidance. Superstition dies hard, but who knows? Possibly a "faith cure" might have resulted, but I have never seen them again to know whether they made the attempt, and if so, with what result.

CHAPTER SEVEN

Stoney Stories

DARTMOOR has the reputation of being the finest natural archaeological museum in this country. Its hillsides are scattered with the remains of prehistoric monuments—stone avenues, single, double or treble; burial kists, menhirs, pounds and circles. The purpose of the stone-box kistvaen is, of course, obvious. That served by the menhirs, avenues and circles remains obscure, a matter of pure guess-work, although most seem to indicate some funerary association.

Avenues of spaced, upright stones extend for yards or miles across the desolate wastes. That on Stall Moor, over two miles in length, claims the distinction of being the longest in the world. Crossing the River Erme, and skirting the Bronze Age village of Erme Pound, its long journey ends upon Green Hill in a burial mound, marked now only by the remains of its retaining circle. Challacombe Down's triple row has been destroyed at one end by tin-mining excavations in Chaw Gully, but that on the north side of Cosdon Beacon leads to a dilapidated retaining circle, containing the unusual feature of a twin, or double kist. Speculation across the centuries may evoke an image of the solemn funeral procession winding its way over the rough heath between the three rows of granite stones— probably newly erected in honour of this special event. The cremated ashes of two important members of the tribe would then be deposited in the double burial chamber at the head of the avenue. There would follow the heaping of moorland turf over the grave forming a round mound of barrow, the newly piled soil being prevented from slipping and washing down by an edging of upright stones—the retaining circle.

The larger stone circles, sometimes called "sacred" circles to distinguish them from the retaining type and those of hut and pound, afford no clue as to their original purpose. Some archaeologists connect them with the ancient pagan sun-worship, their form being representative of the solar disc. Excavations in one or two have revealed charcoal in the centre, possibly from sacrificial, crematory or other ceremonial fires. It seems probable then that these large circles—one or two over 100 feet in diameter—were multi-functional, serving for religious observances, cremations, tribal meetings, rough courts of justice, as suggested in the previous chapter, and ritual festivities including the "ring" dances. Sometimes, outside their circumference, at no great distance, stands a menhir like a tall granite guardian keeping watch. Beside White Moor Circle above Raybarrow Mire the menhir known as White Moor Stone now acts as a boundary mark between three parish commons, those of South Tawton, Throwleigh and Lydford or the Forest, a purpose served by several other menhirs on Dartmoor, including the Longstone on Shuggle Down above Chagford.

Menhirs, as at Drizzlecombe, are also often found in association with stone rows. Yet, of all these oustanding features dating back to antiquity, it seems that—with one or two insignificant exceptions—only the circles have captured popular imagination to the extent of gathering legends into their circumferences. Wherever they are found, whether on Dartmoor, in Cornwall, Wales, Scotland, Ireland or Brittany, the same legend is attached. Almost invariably they are maidens turned into stone for dancing on Sunday, that is to say on the Sabbath, a point to be noted. In this word "Sabbath" we have a most interesting survival, the whole picturesque dancing legend being based, apparently, upon a misinterpretation of that one word.

In her book, *The Witch Cult in Western Europe*, Dr. Margaret Murray describes how the witch covens of medieval England used to appoint as their meeting places well-defined local landmarks. As the "old religion" of the witch-cult was banned in a Christianized country, naturally the rendezvous would be selected in some unfrequented spot—an old oak-tree deep in the wood, a crag upon a wild stream-bank, or one of the ancient stone monuments standing away upon some lonely moorside. Here, long-ago vanished races of men had performed their nature rites in a spirit of belief from which that of the witches now meeting there in later times, differed very little in essentials.

The four annual witch festivals, Candlemas, Beltane, Lammas and Halloween were called *sabbats*, misinterpreted as the more familiar word "Sabbath". As used here, the word has no connection whatever with the Jewish word "Sabbath", being derived from the old French *s'esbattre*, meaning "to frolic". Witches, therefore, whose members included men as well as women, the same term applying to both, went to a stone circle not *on* the *Sabbath*, but *to* a *sabbat*—a significant distinction. As their cult became from necessity more and more of an underground movement, the meaning of the word *sabbat* became gradually forgotten, except among initiates. In its new interpretation it was transferred from the witches' *sabbat* revelry, to the solemn Christian Sabbath or Sunday.

The old stone circles lent themselves conveniently to the typical "ring" formation of the ritual dances, in some of which the participants danced back-to-back. Today many of the old ring dances are in favour again, revived and familiarized as the modern popular Square Dances. In this type of dance, one recurrent figure is that of *dos-si-dos*, in which the performers pass each other *back to back*. A mere detail, but one which links today's square dancers romping beneath the electric lights of a village hall, with those other revellers frolicing by moonlight in the stone circles of long ago.

It must be remembered, also, that witches, whether of yesterday or today, traditionally dance *inside* a circle—if only one that is chalked upon a floor. Strictly, I believe, this should measure nine feet in diameter, that being the most convenient size for accommodating a coven composed of twelve witches and their leader. The latter was usually a man disguised, who led or directed the ritual fertility dances, probably acting as the equivalent of caller in our modern revivals.

Owing to necessary secrecy, as already explained, meetings were held in isolated spots where risk from disturbance was slight. A ring being essential to the ritual, what could be more convenient than an old ready-made circle, well removed from human habitations, away on the wild hillside? That dimensions did not conform to strict standard was immaterial. On the whole, they were near-ideal—except perhaps from the point of view of weather exposure. One of the tall stones would provide a convenient raised seat for the leader, the proximity of a menhir affording an even better elevation. Perched here, in pale moonlight, upon the open, moor, in his horned head-dress disguise, he might well have been mistaken for the devil by any belated moorman. Scurrying homewards down the rough tracks, the man would carry to the village below a hair-raising account of what he believed he had seen—a company of witches (some probably from his own village) dancing in abandoned frenzy round the Devil himself.

According to superstition, at certain specified dates and times, such as midnight, sunrise, noon or midsummer eve, varying in each locality, every stone in a circle becomes endowed with a fleeting moment of life. Then it turns slowly round, or otherwise shifts its position slightly before settling down again into grey immobility. Incidentally, the Rollright Stone Knights of Oxfordshire take quite a long midnight walk to a spring below from which, after indulging in a drink, they march uphill and resume their original places. Does the "king" one wonders, manage to escape from the spiked iron incarceration which protects him from the public, to join his former companions? Or must he watch enviously for ever as they solemnly set forth on their annual outing? It is unusual, by the way, for members of a stone circle, such as these Rollright Knights, to be masculine in character, the majority being the conventional "maidens".

"Then maydes daunce in a ring," wrote Thomas Nash, the Elizabethan poet, and in legend, if not in reality, the "Sabbath"-breaking dancers are almost always feminine. Their male counterparts remained aloof close by in the form of standing-stones or menhirs, which in popular parlance and superstition became "men". Nor is this surprising. Viewed upon a ridge at a distance, a menhir may well be mistaken for a tall human figure against the skyline. More than once when meeting my husband out on the moor, I have been obliged to use binoculars to make certain whether I was heading for a granite menhir or my 6-foot 4-inch husband. Circles and menhirs, maidens and men—even when of stone—are, then, often, although not necessarily, found in company. The White Moor Stone and circle lying in a slight depression between Cosdon Beacon and White Hill have already been mentioned. The 12-foot Longstone beside the Merrivale Circles affords another example.

Often a menhir seems to have been erected in isolation; as a landmark, as a memorial or as some religious symbol, who, at this distance of time can say? The conspicuous figure of 11-foot-tall Beardown Man on the slopes of Devil's Tor, for instance, looms in solitary state with no giddy companions to enliven his age-old vigil. Quentins Man disappeared before living memory but has bequeathed his name to posterity as an indication of his former existence.

The designations *men* and *maidens* have a double significance. *Maen* is Celtic for "stone", our word "long-stone" being an exact translation of *maen-hir*, "stone-long", whence *menhir*. As for the maidens, slur the word slightly, as pronounced in the soft Devon vernacular, and one gets a sound closely approximating to the Celtic *maen*.

Up and down the country, many circles associated with this conventional dancing legend are known as the *Nine Maidens*, irrespective of the actual number of stones comprising the company. The ancient pagan nature religion embraced the special cults of sun and moon. Stone circles to men of the

Bronze Age who erected them may have represented the solar disc by day and been symbolic also of the full moon by night. Latter day witches, practising the old religion of their forbears in exactly the same places, concentrated on the lunar aspect, witches being essentially moon-worshippers, venerating that planet in its three phases, crescent, full and waning. According to T. C. Lethbridge in his book *Witches*, each phase took on a distinct personification resulting in three separate lunar goddesses. Eventually each of these three phases or aspects were again separated into three, creating an image of *nine* moon-goddesses or maidens, each presiding over different occasions and circumstances. It is an extremely interesting complexity which may account for the frequency of the name, not only as applied to stone circles, but found also where other venerated objects stand or once stood—groves of trees, old oaks, or wishing wells. These nine maidens are, of course, another embodiment of the three times three mystic number, seen again in the nine Muses and the nine Valkyries for example.

On Dartmoor a Nine Maidens Circle stands on Watchett Hill just above Belstone. The same idea is echoed faintly again in South Tawton parish where the name Nine Stones has been given to a modern house built upon the fringe of the moor. It is tempting to deduce that the name was not merely a meaningless arbitary choice, but so far no evidence or tradition has come to light by way of elucidation. It is, however, known that this part of the moor was once rich in antiquities that have long since disappeared piecemeal into the walls of the many small "intakes" patterning the north slopes of Cosdon Beacon. Possibly another group of Nine Maidens was among them.

Belstone's Nine Maidens Circle is of the retaining type, originally marking the circumference of a round barrow. A slight depression in the centre indicates the site of a long-vanished kistvaen. The actual number of upright stones at the present time is seventeen. They are small and insignificant, yet somehow in their isolation manage to impart a feeling of true antiquity lacking in some of the larger circles that have—in some cases—"suffered" restoration. Some of the stones have fallen, while gaps indicate where others have been purloined. For some strange reason it is surprisingly difficult to make an accurate count of stones in any circle at the first attempt. From this—literally—unaccountable disability arises the superstition that no two counts ever give the same result.

Eden Phillpotts in his *Book of Avis* reduces the Belstone maidens to seven, although one must conclude that if this number resulted from a personal count, the author must indeed have been badly pixylated or otherwise mysteriously deluded on that occasion. However, he commemorates them in a charming little verse:

> And now at every Hunters Moon
> That haggard cirque of stones so still
> Awakens to immortal thrill,
> And seven small maids in silver shoon
> 'Twixt dark of night and white of day
> Twinkle upon the sere old heath
> Like living blossoms in a wreath,
> Then shrink again to granite grey.
> So blue-eyed Dian shall ever dance
> With Linnette, Bethkin, Jennifer,
> Avisa, Petronell and Nance.

Nine, seven or seventeen, each maiden comes to life—according to Eden Phillpotts—at every Hunter's Moon. Since his numbers also differ from reality possibly he was confusing the Belstone maidens with those of another circle. The version I have always heard is that all shift their positions very slightly each day at noon. Seeing their stocky grey figures through a pulsating summer heat such as we are occasionally favoured with on the high moor, one can at times almost swear to definite, stealthy movement taking place among these quiet stones.

The three largest stone circles on Dartmoor, those of the Two Grey Wethers and Scorhill, rather surprisingly perhaps have no dancing stories attached to them. The very old Chagford legend in which all three appear (as related in the last chapter) is of a much more sombre character. The Grey Wethers, however, figure in one of the standard type tales, which, unlike the Chagford one, is not peculiar to Dartmoor. I have met a similar story in the Lake District where it is told about the Herdwick sheep of the northern fells. In each case the basic idea is identical, being founded upon a practical joke.

According to the Dartmoor version, a novice moorland farmer, wishing to "run" sheep on the hills, went to market to purchase a suitable flock. Having been persuaded into buying two flocks, he was told that he would find them already on Sittaford Tor. Transport difficulties would thus be conveniently solved at the same time. In due course, riding up to inspect his new purchase, the man certainly found two groups of Grey Wethers in the exact spot indicated, but not in the woolly guise that he had been led to expect. Here the story ends abruptly, without sequel, but its origin is very apparent.

It is extraordinary how ovine Dartmoor boulders and stones can appear at a distance to moormen who are hunting for their flocks, and conversely how deceptively granite-like are the rounded backs of the genuine grey wethers and ewes in their weather-patched fleeces as they graze among the rocks. Sittaford is a grassy hill, favoured for this reason by the innumerable sheep that dot its slopes. The story's locale is therefore well chosen.

Possibly owing to their ovine character, the Grey Wethers stones are no dancers, but they do conform to convention in the matter of exercise, taking a short stroll each morning at sunrise. As may be inferred from the Chagford legend, at one time most of the stones in both Grey Wethers circles had fallen but were re-erected at the end of the last century by Baring-Gould and his antiquarian associates Robert Burnard and the two Worths, father and son. Restoration, no matter how carefully carried out, inevitably imparts an air of slight modernization, and the regularity of these stones as they now stand does detract slightly from that genuine air of indefinable antiquity.

The Grey Wethers, lying close together on the lower slopes of the tor, are actually the two largest circles on the moor, Scorhill being third in size. Owing, however, to their rather confined position just outside the stone wall of an enclosure, they appear less imposing than Scorhill, the stones of the latter being so well spaced and placed in a wider, more open, situation. There has been no attempt at restoration here, nor has one heard that the individual members of the ring indulge in exercise of any sort. The circle has, however, acquired the reputation of being in some way eerie. I know several people who say that they are unable to ride their horses along the old track that winds right through it. Their mounts become restive and evince such unwillingness to pass inside the circumference that a detour has to be made, and the track regained on the farther side.

Even older in time than Scorhill and the Grey Wethers circles is Spinster's Rock near Drewsteignton. This ancient monument is not a rock, but four huge granite slabs representing the only recognizable remains of a dolmen or cromlech now left in Devon. Once covered by the usual long barrow, it was a neolithic burial chamber, similar in conception to, but altogether larger than the later Bronze Age kists under their round barrows. Serving rather in the capacity of a family vault than of an individual tomb, the sides were constructed of several great slabs in place of the single stones used for a kist-vaen. Three only of these supports beneath the capstone of Spinster's Rock now remain, and they are not in their original positions. Like most of the ancient monuments, the "Rock" has suffered depredation. The removal one by one, of the side slabs finally brought about a collapse, followed by subsequent restoration in 1862 when the imposts or uprights were replaced incorrectly. Once upon open moorland, Spinster's Rock now stands in a private field belonging to Shilstone Farm, a place owing the name it has retained since the Domesday survey to the shelf or capstone of the cromlech. There are other Shilstones, usually situated around Dartmoor's borders which now exist in name only, no trace remaining of the dolmens that must once have been there.

According to legend the Drewsteignton monument owes its existence to three spinsters who were not necessarily maiden ladies, but spinsters in the sense used by Shakespeare, when, in *Twelfth Night,* he speaks of the "spinsters and the knitters in the sun". The ladies were spinners in the days of Devon's flourishing wool trade when every parish possessed its woollen mills wherever any of Devon's many small streams could be harnessed to turn them. Cottage families were all engaged in the trade, spinning, carding and weaving in thier own homes, the finished work being collected by agents known as "jobblers". Setting out one morning before breakfast to take their spun wool to one of these jobblers, the three stalwart ladies found themselves with a few minutes to spare. To fill in time and enjoy a little healthy exercise before settling down again to their spinning wheels, they amused themselves by setting up the great granite slabs, as they might a house of cards. Wool in its pristine form is still connected with the dolmen, for heavily fleeced sheep today seek shade and shelter under its protective stones.

Another rather confused story relates that a mysterious old man accompanied by his three sons descended from the hills one day, erected the monument in a combined effort, and equally mysteriously disappeared. Some say that the old man was Noah with his three sons, all of them, in common with so much else on Dartmoor, having been turned into stone, the capstone representing Noah, and the imposts the three sons. Shem, Ham and Japheth it would seem, are thus obliged to support their father's extremly old age in perpetuity.

Hansford Worth in his book *Dartmoor* refers to some obscure religious sect known as the Arkites who saw the cromlech as an Arkite cell, Bradmere Pool as a reminder of the "waters that covered the earth" in the Deluge, and the waste mounds whose excavation formed the pool as a miniature Mount Ararat. Whether the Arkite theory developed from the Noah legend or the latter from the former, I have been unable to discover. Certainly here we have a real confusion of folklore. To add to it still further, it might be suggested that, presuming the *three* imposts to be of long enough standing, the three spinsters are representative again of the three moon-maidens. A conspicuous feature such as this ruined burial chamber would be a typical rendezvous for devotees of the old religion, as were the circles.

The three hefty spinsters of the Rock form part of a prehistoric burial chamber. Among certain primitive peoples great stones were erected over a burial, but not necessarily to keep the corpse safely battened down as in the case of Squire Cabell. The idea was that to prevent the spirit of the deceased from arising and becoming a troublesome ghost, it should be provided with a solid and permanent abiding place. Hence, doubtless, arose the idea that such stones, although deeply implanted, were not altogether as immobile as appearance suggested, but at certain seasons, times or dates they indulged in furtive spells of animation. The old wayside Stumpy Cross between Moreton Hampstead and North Bovey is said to revolve slowly three times when Moreton church clock chimes midnight.

CHAPTER EIGHT

More Stoney Stories

AFTER the active stone "maidens", what about the stone "men" of Dartmoor?

Circles of upright stones inevitably attract greater attention than does one lone menhir, unless, like Beardown Man, it is particularly conspicuous. The tall "men" of Drizzlecombe are fine fellows as they stride solemnly along beside the new-born Plym. But, as far as I know, they figure in no story, nor take part in any sort of mild activity. The Longstone on Shuggle, Shovel or Shuffle Down above Chagford, surrounded by a remarkable group of antiquities, has, on the other hand, impressed itself rather more on the popular imagination— probably because more easily accessible. It has been accorded the reputation of pivoting slowly round at sunrise, warming each cold granite face in turn. Possibly this is in compliment to the Grey Wethers who perform the same rite on Sittaford Tor, not so far away, overlooking Shuffle Down.

The village of Sticklepath, tucked into the Taw valley at the foot of Cosdon Beacon, possesses two smaller menhirs. They stand on either side of the A30 trunk road, separated now by the roar and rattle of incessant traffic along what was once a quiet unfrequented track.

The first, sometimes incorrectly described as a cross, is an incised menhir, placed at the foot of the school path behind the Ladywell. It was knocked down and moved from its original position when the present main road was constructed in 1829. Here, in the shade of a young oak and an old crab-apple tree, the incisions are difficult to decipher and no antiquarian has, as yet, explained their significance. In strong sunlight, however, two St. Andrew's crosses and an hour-glass figure may be traced, plus a government broad-arrow from a recent road survey.

The second menhir, kown as the Honest Man stands on a tiny grass patch at the top of Sticklepath Hill. The incisions on its surface are now almost indecipherable as the old stone sinks lower and lower into the ground among encroaching vegetation. A St. Andrew's cross can be traced again here on one face, with faint markings resembling a circle and a crescent—a significant symbolic connection—upon another.

My own theory is that the incised characters on both these stones may be read as records in time. Both are ancient menhirs, left, as were many, in their original positions to serve as signposts. The Incised stone indicates where the track from Belstone joined the old highway; the Honest Man shows where the Mariner's Way branched off on its tortuous route to Sampford Courtenay and the North Devon coast. The Incised stone bears an hour glass or figure eight—the symbols are identical—the latter a mystic sign used in the witches' religion, being therefore possibly cut upon the menhir sometime during the Middle Ages. At a later date still came the addition of a St. Andrew's Cross, a probable reminder that Sticklepath's chantry-chapel, only 100 yards from the menhir, was, and still is, an appendage of the mother church of St. Andrew at Sampford Courtenay. The present day has been productive of the broad arrow—to puzzle future antiquarians.

Much the same sequence of events is, in my opinion, recorded upon the Honest Man which began its long life as a Bronze Age menhir of unknown purpose. Later it served as a signpost, probably also as a meeting place for pagan worshippers who placed the sun-disc and crescent moon upon one side. Christianity added St. Andrew's cross to the stone which incidentally also points the way to Sampford Courtenay's church dedicated to that saint. This seems to me an interesting, and by no means improbable sequence of events.

Two very different stories account for the Honest Man's complimentary name. One feels that only the most eccentric mariners would ever have *chosen* to journey from Dartmouth, right across Devon, to Bideford or Barnstaple by the circuitous and unlikely path traditionally allotted to them and known as the Mariner's Way. In following it, a mariner would have had to walk the roughest open tracts of Dartmoor; cross rivers on precarious stepping-tones, often submerged; wander through fields and churchyards, and squelch through the mud of farmyards and rough lanes. Small wonder that he turned in at any little alehouse that lay along his way, for badly-needed refreshment.

According to legend, one of these mariners, having over-refreshed himself at the Sticklepath inn, lost his 'way' in the wilds of Sticklepath Hill above the village. Looking for the 'signpost' or for someone to direct him, he peered through the darkness and to his joy espied a figure ahead. In his relief he threw his arms round it, embracing what turned out to be the solid granite form of the menhir, and inquired: 'Be you an honest man?' And so the stone was named.

The second explanation of its name is more respectable in character. It relates how, in these same wilds, a traveller was set upon by thieves who robbed him of his purse. Fortunately for him, at the crucial moment a good Samaritan happened to ride up. He routed the footpads, rendered first-aid and restored his purse to the victim, after which this self-effacing rescuer rode off without disclosing his identity. The traveller, impressed by such disinterestedness and presumably having recovered his strength, found and set up the stone on the spot, in commemoration of so honest a man.

The natural wild elements, wind, water and frost, have worn Dartmoor's rock piles into many fantastic forms suggestive of man's agency in their shaping. Indeed, during the last century, when the Druidic theory was at its height, some of the more grotesque, stone figures such as the "Colossi" on Staple Tors, the "sphinx" of Vixen Tor, and Bowerman's Nose were considered to have been the work of the ubiquitous and busy white-robed priesthood.

Of all Dartmoor's stone gentlemen, surely the most grotesque is Bowerman's Nose standing majestically upon Hayne Down near Manaton and presenting an extraordinary silhouette when viewed over the hedge from a certain point on the road leading to the village.

Bowerman is the hard core of a small tor, now lying in a clitter of fallen rock around his feet. Weathering of the granite cracked his protecting shell and he eventually emerged in his present form like a chicken from an egg. With grey cap pushed well back from a face consisting mainly of the parrot-like feature which gives him his name, if ever a figure invited legend it is Bowerman. Yet, apart from one mythical murmer, no story emanates from this oddest of "men". Any old fantasies that surely must once have existed, are now concealed for ever in Bowerman's granite bosom. All that can be said about him with certainty is that Druids were in no way responsible for what has been fashioned entirely by nature, and that in the name we once more meet the Celtic *maen*. Bowerman is—or rather was— *vawr-maen*, the "great stone". Somebody added the "nose" for obvious reasons; not we hope because he bore any resemblance to a completely mythical Norman bow-man who, according to a misty scrap of folklore, settled on a nearby moorland farm after the Conquest.

Some of the great granite boulders have weathered into the piled parallel layers, geologically described as "lamellar", appearing thus as solid lumps upon Waterton Tor, curiously resembling a battleship in shape. Chat Tor, Blackingstone and other hills.

On the moor behind Sourton village lies Corn Ridge which forms part of Sourton Common. Upon its plateau-like summit, among thickly scattered rocks, are two outstandingly large rounded boulders of lamellar formation, known as Branscombe's Loaf and Cheese. In the legend accounting for this name, once again we find a real character, like Drake or Lady Howard, inserted as the central figure of a fictitious tale.

Walter Branscombe or Bronscombe was Bishop of Exeter during the thirteenth century. He was a good and enlightened prelate, who, according to tradition, made a point of paying pastoral visits to his far-flung human flock out in the wilds of Dartmoor. This necessitated long journeys on horseback hence, doubtless, his sympathetic abolition of the terrible funeral treks along the Lych Way when ecclesiastical custom decreed that every interment must take place at the deceased's own parish church. As the whole of Dartmoor Forest lies in Lydford parish, making it the largest parish in England, it was to far-away Lydford that these nightmare funeral processions were directed.

One summer evening the Bishop accompanied by a servant was riding home from one of these formidable pastoral visitations. Exhausted after their long day, they were hot, hungry and thirsty, but encouraged by the fact that they would soon be descending from the rough moorland to the slightly more negotiable track below—the road that is now the main A386 arterial highway between Tavistock and Okehampton. As they crossed Corn Ridge on this last lap of their journey a stranger, seeming to rise up out of the heather, suddenly appeared beside their horses. Noting their exhaustion, he solicitously offered them some refreshment from the wallet he carried. The unsuspecting Bishop accepted with grateful alacrity, whereupon the stranger extracted a little round loaf and a lump of cheese. *But*, most fortunately, at that crucial moment, the servant happened to catch a glimpse of cloven hoofs beneath the stranger's long travelling cloak, which, hot evening though it was, he was nevertheless wearing—perhaps to disguise his identity. With great presence of mind, the servant dashed the food from his master's hand just as his lordship was about to take a bite. The cheese flew in one direction, the bread in another, and there they are still on Corn Ridge today, transformed into two great rounded granite boulders, distinguishable from the others all around by their huge size.

One wonders what long-forgotten incident in folklore memory once occurred upon this unfrequented and in no way remarkable moorland ridge, that it should have been selected as the scene of the Bishop's temptation. The imaginative and inquiring mind might, perhaps, try to find some connecting link between "corn" and "loaf", but unavailingly, the word "corn" here being merely a corruption of "crown", referring to the high or "crowning" ridge. The story itself is clearer and better defined than many others; it is the chosen locality that constitutes something of a puzzle.

The picturesque Moretonhampstead area is dotted with small moorland outcrops in the form of heather-clad, rock-crowned hills. Nattadon, Meldon, Pepperdon, Hingstone Rocks, Hel Tor and Blackingstone stand like islands above a sea of cultivation and enclosure, their rocky composition having defeated the ploughs of many centuries. All are now picnic and viewing spots for the general public. The lamellar lumps of Hel Tor and Blackingstone, reminiscent in shape of Branscombe's Loaf and Cheese, figure in another of Dartmoor's standard type legends.

According to this, these two hills were once mere moor eminences, lacking their crowning rocks. Then one day King Arthur, standing upon Hel Tor, engaged in a hurling match with the Devil, stationed upon Blackingstone. Quoits hurtled backwards and forwards until royalty finally emerged victorious. The Devil, angry at defeat, immediately performed another of his ossifying transformations. The two quoits, now turned into stone, lie where he left them, appearing today as the small crowning tors of Hel and Blackingstone. This same story is told, with local variations, in many other places, including, as might be expected, Cornwall.

One day some years ago, my husband and I were standing in a lane near Tintagel, in which neighbourhood, of course, King Arthur performed many feats. On the grass verge lay yet another of these fabled stone "quoits" at which we had paused to look. Footsteps passed behind us and a voice, without any

preamble, remarked caustically: "And *that* b'aint true neither."
With which cryptic utterance the Cornishman continued on his
way without another word.

As accessible as Blackingstone or Hel Tor, and so equally
well known, is the Coffin Stone lying beside a grassy track on
the road down to Dartmeet. Actually "the stone" is composed
of two contiguous granite slabs, upon which it was customary
for weary bearers to rest their burden when carrying a coffin
for burial in Widecombe churchyard following Bishop
Branscombe's merciful dispensation. Here the funeral party
halted for much-needed rest and refreshment in the form of a
picnic meal, the coffin being placed meanwhile upon this
particular stone. During this interval the party sometimes
whiled away a few minutes by incising the small crosses that
can be seen today, cut upon the granite surface—a reminder
of the stone's original purpose. Tradition has it that the two
rocks, originally one, were cleft by a thunderbolt when the
coffin of an unusually wicked character was rested there on his
last journey.

F

CHAPTER NINE

The Old River Gods

DARTMOOR possesses innumerable rivers and streams, a few pools of artificial origin, but no lakes in the usual meaning of the term apart from modern reservoirs. Devon has more running water than any other county in England, but it *is* running. There are no still mountain tarns and meres as in the Lake District, and nothing equivalent to the Surrey "ponds". The word "lake" certainly appears on maps but these "lakes" are but the trickling tributaries of the Dartmoor rivers near their sources. Such are Drylake, Redlake, Dead Lake and Harlake. The name is of Scandinavian derivation, akin to "leak" and "leat". Indeed, in our Dartmoor village today some of the older inhabitants invariably refer to the mill-leat which runs parallel to the A30 highway, as the *leak*. So upon Dartmoor, our lakes are not static, but flowing.

The few pockets of still water have been artificially excavated being usually the flooded pits of old mine-workings. Possibly because they are so few, most of the pools seem to be regarded with a certain amount of superstitious awe by countryfolk. Few South Tawton villagers, for instance, care to take the short cut through the old limestone quarries there after dusk. Here three picturesque pools have been formed in abandoned excavations, now beautified by ever-insidious nature. One pool in particular lying at the foot of an almost sheer cliff bears a sinister reputation from the fact that a runaway horse and cart from the field above now lie at the bottom of the pool, whose depth, like so many others, is said to be unfathomable. More than one suicide has also been committed in its rather sinister dark-green water.

Similar in origin to those at South Tawton is the Meldon Quarry Pool near Okehampton, an eerie, tree-shadowed piece of water suggesting and receiving suicide. In 1936, after one such tragedy when the body could not be located, the old practice of "singing for a drowned body" was resorted to and enacted upon the spot. A choir from Okehampton being collected, a service with prayers and the requisite singing was conducted by the water's edge. *A week later*, so said my informant, the body was recovered—hardly proof of the ceremony's efficacy.

A variation of this custom was to float a loaf of bread weighted with mercury upon the surface of the water. It was believed that where the loaf sank the drowned body would be found. This course was seriously advocated in 1955 when the clay pools near Bovey Tracey were being dragged unavailingly for a woman's body.

Yet another piece of still water formed by mining excavation is Bradmere or Bradford Pool near Drewsteignton. When being mined for tin in former days, by the Chagford Stannators, it was known as Shilstone Venn, deriving its name from the "shelf"-stone of Spinster's Rock from which it is separated only by a narrow lane. *Venn*, Devonshire vernacular for "fen", describes the boggy nature of the ground all round the gateway giving access to the pool. When and why the picturesque old name was superseded by the undistinguished Bradmere or Bradford, seems to be unrecorded.

The pool lies gloomily amidst crowding trees which darken its three acres of water except on a hot, still, sunny Midsummer Day. Then their reflections on the breathless surface are so vivid that it is difficult to tell where earth-trees merge into water-woods. Several superstitious tales emanate from this leaf-enclosed spot. The Noah-Arkite legend has already been mentioned. When Druidical theories were rife, Spinster's Rock became the ruins of a Druid's temple, and the pool its "sacred" lake used for purification ceremonies. There are old rumours of an underground passage joining the pool to the River Teign and emerging near the Tolmen, a story neatly linking all three antiquities if one includes the "sacred lake". Even today the existence of a subterranean passage is still spoken of, but with growing uncertainty, usually prefaced by "they say". Possibly a semi-submerged entrance to some adit from the old pit formed the basis of this belief.

Although Bradmere Pool is now recognized for what it is—a tin-mining excavation with banks formed by the spoil-heaps, it retains the reputation of being haunted. Only a year or so ago, I was told by a young woman that it was haunted, but exactly by *what* seems to be another of these half-remembered or half-forgotten folk memories. Her description was:

"It's as if there's something in there that makes you want to throw yourself into the water."

That was the extent of her knowledge, and of her own personal reactions, but it was nevertheless a revealing remark.

A variation of the same superstition is attached to yet another abandoned and flooded tin-mine out on the moor between Sheepstor and Princetown. This pool is known variously as Crazywell, Classiwell or Classenwell. With the exception of a few summer hikers, or young people undertaking "endurance tests", practically nobody walks the rougher Dartmoor tracks today. Formerly those who did, returning from work in the quarries and peat-ties, or from rounding up cattle, would make a detour of several miles rather than pass anywhere near Crazywell Pool at dusk. For then, in the moaning of the wind over the stark acre of water a ghostly voice might be heard calling the name of the next person who would die in the neighbourhood; there was always the dread of hearing one's own name thus fatally pronounced.

As with so many sheets of water whose level varies little, Crazywell enjoyed the reputation of such fathomless depth that the bell-ropes of Walkhampton church tied together failed to touch the bottom. However, according to J. L. W. Page, one excessively dry summer exploded the myth. Water had to be "borrowed" and when pumped out, revealed the fathomless hollow to be about 15 feet in depth. Now the waters are restored and lie darkly shadowed by the high encircling banks of its one-time spoil.

An interesting fragment of folklore connects Crazywell with Piers Gaveston, the effete favourite of Edward II. During his eclipse and exile from Court, he is said to have visited the pool to consult the prophetic voice about his own subsequent fate. Any link between Piers Gaveston and a remote Dartmoor pool may seem at first as surprising as the site of the Black Prince's tomb on Cosdon Beacon. Then one recalls that at one time this nobleman held the lucrative wardenship of the Stannaries, the unique organization that for centuries legislated for the tin trade of Dartmoor. Nevertheless, his name in this connection is certainly an anachronism of later interpolation. In the fourteenth century, tin-mining was flourishing and Crazywell would not then have been abandoned and flooded as it is now. Unless, therefore, there was previously some small natural pool there, one can find no explanation for Gaveston's memory having stamped itself upon this particular spot. Apparently not even Devon-born, velvet-cloaked Sir Walter Raleigh, a later warden, left as indelibile an impression upon the tough Dartmoor tinners, in spite of having raised their wages from 2s. to 4s. per week, as did the worthless Piers Gaveston, for some unknown reason.

Unaccustomed as he was to them in general, the primitive Devonian *may* have found something unnaturally sinister about still waters. It was once considered most unlucky, if not fatal, to see one's own image reflected in water. In ancient belief, this replica was in fact an integral part of the living person that had somehow escaped from the confining body; it was his inner self or soul. If this image could be seen by the unwitting projector, this part of him was *there*, in the water. Logically it followed that it might also be seen and possibly captured by some enemy, reducing the living body to an empty soul-less husk. We get one aspect of this old belief in the Greek story of Narcissus who, leaning over a clear pool, saw reflected in it his second self which insidiously lured him to his death by drowning.

Undoubtedly in these Dartmoor echoes we have the lingerings of very ancient superstition, appearing in the folklore of many lands. Undine, the water-sprite, materializing from a spring, wept her faithless husband to death. Melusine was another water-maiden who married a mortal. Then there were the Lorelei, fatal maidens of the Rhine; King Arthur's Lady of the Lake; the water-nixy claiming the miller's first-born in German fairy-tale; even the cold, dripping mermaid enticing her human lover into her ocean home. All are direct ancestors of the vague compulsions and voices of Dartmoor's waters. If such insubstantial beings possess even paler wraiths, surely they linger in such places as Bradmere, Crazywell and Lydford Gorge where the slender 123-foot high waterfall bears the eponymous name of "The White Lady".

These white ladies again have their origin in the Great White Goddess Diana of the Moon, presiding deity of the old nature worship, not only in ancient Greece, but also in Britain, yesterday and today. She appeared in many guises, particularly that of the water sprite, and to realize how easily these wraiths materialized from spring and waterfall it is, rather oddly perhaps, only necessary for example to visit the modern, newly built city centre in Coventry today. Here, one of the fountains rises and falls in a tall, shapely cascade. Transfer it to a wild, lonely valley or to a tumbling moorland stream at dusk or by moonlight, and a very convincing white lady, her draperies billowing in the wind, would rise up before one.

Lydford Gorge also hides in its depths, the haunted pool known as Kit's Steps, where another cascade falls over the rocks. Beside the pool at its foot, the apparition of old Kitty, her head bound in a red kerchief, may sometimes be seen. Being presumably of exemplary character, she has not been "black-dogged" like Weaver Knowles, whose particular pool-haunting has already been described. Kitty has retained her human semblance. Was she "called" by the white lady? Or did she, as tradition relates, merely slip and fall to her death one evening on her way home from market? Such an accident would surprise no one who has slithered along the narrow, slippery paths of the gorge after rain. Etymologists, however, have a habit of exploding pleasing little tales of romance and tradition. According to them, "Kit" is merely a corruption of the word "skit" denoting broken, scattered rock, a term found in other Dartmoor place names such as Skit Bottom near Hartor. Certainly there is no lack of jagged rock at Skits Steps and Pool, but whether the unfortunate Kitty, in spite of the etymologists, nevertheless fell in and was drowned there, who can now say?*

The Undines, water-sprites, white ladies and naiads all claimed their human sacrifices either directly or indirectly. In former days the victim was despatched to the gods unwillingly. In later, more moderate times the offering became voluntary or even accidental. Today we find the kernel of the same primitive idea lingering in the still often-quoted, if not now actually believed saying, that the River Dart annually demands a human life:

> Dart, Dart, cruel Dart,
> Every year thou claim'st a heart.

Or, more simply:

> Dart, Dart,
> Wants a Heart.

The "cry of the Dart" is a very old Dartmoor superstition. At certain times, the unusually loud and insistent noises of the river, especially where it rushes round the Broad Stone, was construed into the "voice" calling for its "heart".

William Crossing tells the story of a farm lad from nearby Rowbrook who became obsessed with the notion that he was the river's next destined victim. One night, shouting: "Dart's calling me" he ran out into the darkness down towards the river and was never seen or heard of again.

* See Postscript, *Kit's Steps*, p. 190

Beatrice Chase, who had much of the mystic in her character, sent me an account of one of her personal experiences of
this belief. From her Widecombe cottage one summer day, she
herself became aware of the "cry" of the Dart, which, she
wrote, "chilled and frightened" her, being an unusual sound at
that time of the year. (This, incidentally, was a more or less
tantamount admission that the phenomenon is governed by
meteorological conditions.) At the time, being an ardent Roman
Catholic, she was troubled about a neighbour's newly-born
child, not yet baptized. She sensed that the river was about to
claim that particular young heart and reflected that it must
surely be the first occasion on which the Dart had "cried for
a heart" within the hour of a child's birth. Once convinced of
this, she characteristically set about trying to remedy the
situation as she saw it, by finding a priest to perform the
baptism immediately. But it was not soon enough and the
baby was found dead in its cot before the ceremony could take
place.

That is one modern instance of belief in this age-old idea of
the fatal call of the river gods. Another recent story, less
definite in detail, comes from Belstone.

A few years ago, an elderly native of the place told how, one
evening, he was walking along the West Cleave beyond the
village, when he saw a farmer-neighbour standing below him
on the brink of the rapidly flowing East Okement river. Sensing
impending tragedy, he hurried down the slope to join him. As
he did so, he heard a loud voice, apparently emanating from
the turbulent water, distinctly proclaim the words: "The hour
has come, but not the man."

This fragmentary story again lacks detail that one would so
much like to know, but it is undoubtedly related to the same
"call of the river" theme. It is, however, unique in its inference,
which seems to be that for some reason, the wrong victim was
presenting himself and was being rejected. It is the only
instance of the kind which I have heard, and is particularly
interesting as being of present-day occurrence. I might add that,

knowing the narrator, superstitious imagination is the last thing of which he might have been suspected.

When native moormen or strangers travelled the Dartmoor ways and were obliged to cross the swollen streams more often than now, drowning accidents were not infrequent. The Dart, divided into two branches, East and West before their union at Dartmeet, drains a larger area than any other Dartmoor river. It might, therefore, justifiably be considered more accident-prone perhaps than any of the other streams. Apart from this, plus the fact that "Dart" and "heart" form a convenient doggerel rhyme, there seems to be no reason why this long-persisting superstition should have clung more firmly to the Dart than to any other river.

The River Taw flows through our own village, dividing our garden from the moorland. At times, its swift passage as it winds down from the hills, is more audible than at others. Then the older, still weather-wise country-folk say: "The river's crying. It's going to rain." In this case, the watery voice has degenerated—like the green woodpecker's note—into a mere, but incidentally fairly accurate, weather prophecy from which a few logical conclusions may be drawn. Sound carries more clearly when the wind is in a certain quarter. That quarter indicates approaching storm conditions when rivers rise in swift and sudden spate and tragedy may result to humans or cattle. On Dartmoor in this way and others, the "hearts" of many beasts are annually sacrificed to the unrelenting old river gods.

Among other places where similar customs prevail, the villages of Holne and Kingsteignton each hold an annual ram-roasting feast, survival of ancient pagan festivals when blood sacrifices were offered to the sun and other nature gods to stimulate fertility. The season at which these celebrations are held is indicative of their origin. Holne celebrates at midsummer, Kingsteignton at Whitsun, a time of year when nature's abundant fertility becomes apparent.

It is on record, however, that upon one occasion Kingsteignton's annual feast coincided with a drought, when the village
water supply failed. Legend here interpolates that there was
not water enough even to perform an urgent baptism. A ram
was therefore sacrificed on the bed of the dry water-course. Its
revitalizing blood seeped through the stones and gravel, presumably to the comatose form of the river-spirit somewhere
below. The effect was miraculous. Water started to bubble up
instantaneously and the child was baptized, a stone in the
stream-bed still bearing the imprints of the mother's fingers as
she leaned upon it with one hand, holding her baby over the
rising water with the other. "And after that," says the old
record tersely, "it rained."

Thus the resuscitation of both sun and river god is combined
in the folk-memory of Kingsteignton's Whitsuntide fair.

Few of Dartmoor's superstitious traditions can be more
deeply rooted in the past than these remnants of ancient nature-
worship, still practised in other countries today as *voodoo*. In
Haiti, for example, crowds of natives gather to hold a mass ceremonial to their river god, who, in guise of a snake, lives in a
waterfall. Even more striking evidence is seen in their offerings
to a sea-god—counterpart of Neptune. Wreaths of flowers,
images and fruit, substitutes for one-time human sacrifice, are
thrown into the sea, while the deity is invoked. If the invocation
is successful, the god then takes possession of one or more of
his devotees, who fall into frenzied trances, having to be forcibly
restrained from throwing themselves into the water. This
attempt at self-immolation in religious observance thousands of
years old is strangely, but surely, echoed by the twentieth
century "callings" of strange voices from Dartmoor pool or
river.

Apart from the Dart, folklore has nothing of import to tell
about other Dartmoor rivers, or rather perhaps, nothing has
survived. There is a so-called "legend" personifying the rivers
Tamar, Tavy and Torridge which is obviously a modern concoc-
tion, created by someone "all in one piece" as a little fairy tale.

"Giant Dartmoor," the nymph Tamara, and her lovers Tavy and Torridge are *ersatz* inventions, having nothing to do with the genuine "old tale". The story is in the same category as another I have read describing the machinations of the Witch of Vixen Tor. This character certainly has no affinity with the true witches and witchcraft of Devon whose ways are described in later chapters. There is something definitely "phoney" about both these mis-termed "legends" which are completely out of keeping with traditional Dartmoor.

CHAPTER TEN

Haunts

MANY waters need many bridges and Devon has as varied a collection of these as any county in Britain. Narrow moorland streams such as the North Teign above Chagford and its tributary the Walla Brook, are crossed by single granite slabs of colossal dimensions, known as "clappers". Cyclopean bridges of two or three slabs resting on rough stone piers take the place of clappers where the river width is too great for a single span. The old Post-bridge is the most outstanding example of this type surviving today. The ruins of those at Dartmeet, Bellever and Knack Mine now lie immersed among the river bed boulders. Cottagers have their individual foot-slabs over the brooklets that still flow down many village streets in front of their doorsteps. There are beautiful medieval structures such as Fingle, and farther away, the famous long bridges of Bideford and Barnstaple. Newest and most imposing of all is the modern suspension bridge alongside Brunel's, crossing the River Tamar, which, by the way, claimed its quota of "hearts" during construction when several fatal accidents occurred.

Some of the older, less-frequented bridges are reputedly haunted. More are not. Where they occur, the most usual "haunts" are of the black dog or Devil type, not, as might perhaps be expected, white ladies and water sprites. Flowing down from Raybarrow Mire below Cosdon Beacon, the picturesque little Blackaton Brook reaches Gidleigh parish. Here in the maze of narrow moorland lanes that intersect the district, it is crossed by a little stone bridge upon which sounds of desperate fighting may sometimes be heard at night as

Cavaliers and Roundheads reputedly re-enact some of their old encounters in phantom animosity. During the Civil War several skirmishes took place in this neighbourhood, and it was in Chagford that the cavalier Sidney Godolphin was killed in the porch of that old hostelry the Three Crowns Inn.

Now here we have a modern addition, carrying this piece of battle folklore one step further. In 1964 a Throwleigh resident told me that as relatives staying with him were crossing this bridge one evening they became acutely aware of conflict raging all round them. The interesting point is that these percipients received a definite impression that the nature of the unseen struggle was very much older in time than the reputed Civil War period—possibly even a re-enactment of some prehistoric conflict. Not far from this bridge and having the same stream flowing through its grounds stands a house once owned by a friend. On many occasions she was troubled by the appearance, not of a white lady, but of a lady in black with white accessories. So vivid was the materialization that every detail of her dress could be noted; stiff watered black silk, a very short white apron, and a white fichu fastened with an unusually large oval brooch containing a lock of hair. Local inquiry elicited a knowledge of this ghost together with the rumour of a woman having drowned herself there many years ago when the stream was in full spate.

Our friend sold the property, but the new owners put it on the market again almost at once, explaining that the house seemed to contain other inhabitants beside themselves, of whose presence they were constantly aware.

Rather more conventional is the story attached to a small bridge on the River Bovey between Chudleigh and Stover. Here, apparently, some amorphous being still troubles belated travellers. In 1961 a woman living nearby described the "haunt" to me as: "Something waving its arms that runs along-side anyone walking or riding a horse or a bicycle." She could supply no more definite details.

Formerly, when Stover, now a girls' school, was the old home of the Templer family, great difficulty was experienced in keeping servants, neither the young women nor their accompanying swains being willing to cross the bridge at night. My informant added that even today, her seventeen-year-old son riding his motor-cycle avoids that route after dark. It must be a stout-hearted "haunt" indeed to pit itself so perseveringly against the modern high-speeding ton-up youngster.

Newbridge crosses the Teign near the claypits at Chudleigh Knighton. Here, on the heath, Dewer may sometimes be seen ending his nightly excursions. I know one keen angler who never fishes near that spot after dusk. He says simply that it "makes him feel spooky". Some spooks, perhaps, are easily conjured into being. "If Lea Bridge near Bridford Weir is haunted," said another fisherman friend, "I am the Haunt." He then descibed how, having left his car on the bridge while he fished below one night, he happened to slip and fall into the river, getting a good soaking. Dry clothes were in the car, and in bright moonlight he clambered out and changed on the bridge. "Anyone who saw me dancing about, trying to keep warm, and flapping my arms in and out of my shirt, would certainly swear that something exceedingly odd was to be seen on that bridge," he said.

Doubtless many hauntings have as simple an explanation.

On the moorland road between Warren House Inn and Chagford, an area, incidentally, rich in legend and folklore, is a dip between two hills. Here the road almost imperceptibly bridges a tiny trickling stream, one of the head-water tributaries of the Bovey. Rather curiously, this insignificant spot has acquired a sinister reputation. From various sources I had gathered merely that it was haunted, then, a few months ago a woman asked me whether I knew any details about this spot, where she told me she had undergone a strange experience. She is a Dartmoor lover, driving and walking on the moor with her terrier whenever opportunity offers. After one such outing, she was driving home in daylight by this familiar route. As she crossed the little white-railed bridge, she was suddenly assailed by an extraordinary sensation. She became stone-cold, her flesh began to creep, and such violent shudders took possession of her that she was obliged to stop the car. Thinking that she must have become stricken with sudden illness she reached for her coat from the back seat. She then saw that her dog, lying beside it, was crouched shivering in one corner, hackles up, teeth bared, plainly the abject victim of terror. Realization then dawned, that she herself was not suffering this icy chill from illness but from fear—yet of what she had no notion. Pulling herself together, she shot up the hill on the other side then stopped and looked back, trying to find some cause for this unnerving incident. Everything appeared perfectly normal and she decided to drive back over the same ground again to test her reactions. The pitiful state of her terrified dog deterred her, however. She felt it unfair to subject him to a possible repetition of that experience, so drove on, gradually recovering normality. At the first opportunity she drove down into that little bridged hollow again, but without incident. Since then she tells me, she has crossed it several times and all has been as usual, nor, like others who have had similar experiences, can she offer any explanation of the incident.

Recently an ardent cyclist described how, some years ago, when cycling down this same hill, he too, experienced a similar and frightening sensation. He felt as though both he and his machine were disintegrating, and was genuinely surprised to find that once over the bridge he "was still there—all in one piece. I can assure you," he added, "it was not a speed wobble because I know all about that, and I have always been a very steady and careful rider. It was something quite different and very uncanny."

These two accounts are by no means unique. Other people have been similarly affected by curious, indefinable sensations, of which some account is given later.

The white ladies of stream and waterfall are, together with the Devil, black dogs, monks and nuns, among the commonest of apparitions. It is a little puzzling, however, to find them so often transported into houses.

Dartington Hall has a white lady among other ghostly visitants. So also has Baring Gould's old home, Lewtrenchard House. A lady who had the tenancy of this place for some years tells me that she often slept there alone, but no pale lady ever came to trouble her. Yet during the Second World War when the house was used as an army billet, she encountered a white-faced batman one day who stammered out that he "had just seen her". What he then described was a shadowy figure, which at first he took to be some member of the family standing in an archway. Gradually it took on the distinct semblance of a woman, finally vanishing through a wall.

Baring Gould himself related how one evening, hearing the distinct sound of carriage wheels crunching upon the gravel drive, he went out to greet his family on their expected return from a party. When he opened the front door the drive was empty and silent, but from above his head in the darkness there came the sound of a loud mocking laugh. I have heard both sea-gulls and "screech"-owls suggested as an explanation of this ghostly voice. Lewtrenchard is perhaps rather a far cry from the moor, but Baring Gould was so essentially a Dartmoor man that one tends to think of him in that connection.

On the true confines of the moor near Gidleigh, tucked away in a maze of narrow lanes not far from haunted Blackaton Bridge, stands Wonson Manor. It is one of the many pleasant small sub-manor houses to be found in Devon, formerly of some importance, now of none.

Here on the panelling of one of the downstairs rooms is painted a large ace of diamonds. According to tradition, a seventeenth-century owner of the house, in a game of cards, staked all his lands and lost, after which he vowed never to touch a card again. To remind himself of this resolution he had the offending ace painted on the wall where it might always be in view and where it still remains. Possibly he was entertaining a few friends from the nearby army at the time, for sometimes, if the door of that room is opened quietly in the evening, four men in cavalier dress may be seen sitting there with playing cards in their hands. However, any shock sustained downstairs by coming unexpectedly upon these phantom gamblers, is counteracted upon retiring to bed. There, one of the bedrooms is pervaded or invaded by a benign female influence. Whether she is a "white lady" or not cannot be stated for she has never been seen. But the occupant of the bed is conscious of gentle hands smoothing his pillow and "tucking him in" comfortably for the night. There is no hint of further ministrations.

Benignant also were the monks, who, until "asked to leave" haunted a house in the neighbourhood of Bovey Tracey. To avoid publicity, the house again must remain anonymous. The owners bought and installed an old staircase, discarded from Buckfast Abbey. Upon the backs of some of the treads, they found names and initials carved by monks of bygone days. Soon, regularly at the same time every evening, monastic figures were to be seen passing quietly up and down the staircase. They became so much a part of the household's everyday life, that the children used to wait for their ghostly visitors to come and stand beside their beds, with folded hands in an attitude of prayer. Their benign presence was accepted almost with affection until publicity put an end to this unique state of affairs. Inevitably the story got about, the house was beseiged by pressmen, camera-men, men of the B.B.C., and the owners were reluctantly obliged to pass sentence of banishment. Clergy were called in to exorcize these pleasant phantoms which were reverently and successfully "laid", and genuinely missed by the family.

There is a remote hamlet on the borders of Dartmoor, under the ecclesiastical care of a neighbouring parish. Names, again, are withheld by request. Visit the partly twelfth-century primitive little church, step inside and close the heavy door, banishing the outer world. Immediately one becomes conscious of a curious isolation in time. The present seems to be obliterated and one is enveloped in, and somewhat oppressed by a heavy intangible atmosphere from the past.

Scattered around this ancient church are a few old cottages and farmhouses. In one of the latter, a young farmer, his wife and two small children were living during the 1950s, when they began to be troubled by poltergeist manifestations of the usual type, occurring mainly in the bedroom occupied by the two children. This fact naturally aroused suspicion at first, but there seemed to be no doubt that the case was genuine. Fearing ridicule, for some time the couple said nothing, until both were on the verge of a nervous breakdown and the children thoroughly terrified. The farmer then called on the rector asking for his advice and help.

Describing the occasion, the rector told me that he went to the farmhouse one evening after the children had been put to bed elsewhere. He and the parents then entered the troubled room together.

"It was during the short service I held there," said the rector, "that I realized the presence of what seemed to be a strong, malevolent force, doing its best to defeat my efforts."

Apparently the farmer, too, was conscious of this influence, for at the end of the service he asked the rector if he could explain exactly what had been going on, a question which the rector was unable to answer having been completely baffled himself. One result of this spiritual conflict was curious. The rector was left with an acute physical pain down one side of his body which persisted for some hours during which time his left arm remained almost paralysed.

After a break for supper, he went upstairs again to spend the night alone in the haunted room. Everything was quiet and normal, pervaded by a feeling of peace. The poltergeist or other "spirit" had apparently been successfully laid, nor did the family experience any further trouble.

"But," concluded the rector, "I am convinced that the room contained some evil influence from the past. It was the most mysterious experience of my life."

His successor, experiencing his first West Country incumbency, has received several helpful, if overt, hints concerning certain individuals whom it is considered inadvisable to "cross".

More recently, just before Christmas 1963, an exorcizm performed by Dr. Mortimer, Bishop of Exeter, aroused a good deal of local publicity. In the village of Abbotskerswell, an old house, scene of a former suicide, had been converted into flats. One of these, occupied by a young couple, became so disturbed by violent poltergeist activities that they found it impossible to remain there. After thorough investigation, proving that the manifestations were genuine and no hoax, the Bishop conducted a service of exorcizm and sprinkled the rooms with holy water. As in the previous case, peace and normality were immediately restored.

That was not quite the finale however. Shortly afterwards, the Press reported that the ghost, successfully driven from one flat, was now haunting another in the same house where it appeared as the figure of a man dressed in Edwardian clothes —presumably the suicide. There seem to have been no further exorcizm, and there, up to the present, the story ends somewhat abruptly.

The house on Dartmoor, haunted by a phantom pack of hounds, has already been described in Chapter 4. Another allegedly haunted cottage stands in the neighbourhood of Drewsteignton, at a spot locally known as Bloody Corner. Tradition asserts that a murder was once committed here, and that on the anniversary of the dark deed, at midnight, a thin trickle of blood may be seen flowing from under the cottage door down on to the road below.

A mile or so further on in the same vicinity is an innocuous-looking rough pasture field, no different in appearance from others surrounding it. Yet, according to the farmer who owns it, no animal will stay in that field, even for a night. No matter how strong the fencing, horses, cows, pigs or sheep are missing in the morning, having desperately sought and found, or made, some means of escape. Why this should be so remains unexplained, as do the reactions of animals to certain places on the moor, about which more will be said later.

Many houses, from cottage to mansion, have their recognized ghosts, but it is not often that a house itself figures as a phantom. Not far from Haytor, on Dartmoor's eastern edge, is a small estate, with a house that was once the site of a little religious community about which nothing now seems to be remembered. Behind the house lies a sizeable wood, bounded on one side by a public, but unfrequented, lane.

Three or four years ago, a newcomer to the district remarked to the owner that when walking along this lane the previous evening, she had been admiring the charming cottage just visible through the trees of his plantation. Quite nonplussed, he assured her that no cottage existed there, and never had to his knowledge. But, completely incredulous, she insisted that she could not have been mistaken, and went back next evening to verify it. No cottage was visible, and the matter was treated as a mild family joke, it being assumed that the lady was just 'seeing things'.

Some months later, a new bungalow was built in a clearing just opposite. Meeting him one day, the "daughter of the bungalow" inquired whether he were the owner of the pretty little cottage in the wood. She added that she could find no way in to it, and asked whether there was access from another side.

These two totally unconnected "visions" are certainly puzzling. Both ladies were strangers in the district. Neither was acquainted with the other and only knew the landowner well enough by sight, just to "pass the time of day" with him. He was born on the estate, inherited from his father, and has no record of there ever having been a cottage where his well-grown plantation now stands. Nor, after careful search, can he find any traces suggestive of old foundations. It is just possible, but not probable, that a low evening sun striking through the tree-trunks, might create the semblance of a building, but hardly in such picturesque detail as was described by each percipient. Also, if so, the phenomenon would surely have been noted and commented upon previously.

So the phantom cottage remains a mystery, and its owner—if that is the correct expression to apply to a non-existent building—a puzzled man.

A few months after the first edition of this book appeared, I received a visit from an Ordnance Surveyor. He told me that he had just been sent to survey in detail a small area in the Haytor district. Looking down on this terrain from a high vantage point to check his map, he noticed one cottage that he had apparently missed. Smoke was rising from the chimneys and clothes blowing on a line. To remedy the omission he pinpointed and walked down to the exact spot. He toothcombed the vicinity but could find no cottage or trace of any building. Encountering a lady exercising her dog, he enquired where this cottage might be. Her reply surprised him. She, too, had seen it—once—but had never been able to locate it again.

Considerably puzzled, he returned to his lodging where, happening to pick up a copy of this book, he opened and read this chapter. The coincidence was so striking that he called on me next day. I am familiar with that particular locality; he, being a map-maker had, of course, made himself so. We compared notes very carefully, proving with certainty that his vanishing cottage was undoubtedly that described already.

CHAPTER ELEVEN

The White Bird of Oxenham

FROM hauntings by white ladies we pass to hauntings by white birds, or rather to one particular white bird, which seems to have undergone some slight modification during the course of the centuries. Accounts of this death-omen, the White Bird of Oxenham, to my mind form one of the most interesting and at the same time most baffling pieces of folklore tradition to be found in Devon.

In the large, scattered moorland parish of South Tawton lies Oxenham Manor. Originally, like Wonson, a small pleasant manor house, it has now, like so many others of its type and period, degenerated into a rough farm. Once it was the home of the Oxenham family, whose "canting" arms, consisting of three oxen, now swing above the Oxenham Arms Inn in South Zeal, the larger of the two villages comprising South Tawton parish.

Oxenhams were established at the manor in the reign of Elizabeth I, the earliest member of whom we have any account being the merchant adventurer John, who sailed to the Pacific with Drake, and who figures in Kingsley's novel *Westward Ho!* There was a tradition in the Oxenham family, old even then, that the death of one of its members was often foretold by the apparition of a white bird. In the oldest accounts this bird is described as white-crested. Then it became white-breasted, and finally plain white. The phantom was not confined to the manor house itself, but might appear to a doomed Oxenham wherever he happened to be living. There are vouched-for records of its periodical manifestations from the seventeenth to the present century.

One of the earliest accounts was published in the reign of Charles I, when a gentleman named James Howell noticed in a London stone-cutter's shop a large marble memorial or grave stone. The inscriptions upon it struck him as being so remarkable that he copied and published them. The first three read as follows:

Here lies John Oxenham, a goodly young man, in whose chamber as he was struggling with the pangs of death, a Bird with a white breast was seen fluttering about his bed, and so vanished.

Here also lies Mary Oxenham, the sister of the said John, who died the next day, and the same Apparition was seen in the Room.

Here lies, hard by, James Oxenham, the son of the same John, who died a child in his cradle a little after, and such a Bird was seen fluttering about his head a little before he expired, which vanished afterwards.

And these three were followed by a fourth, that of Elizabeth, John's mother, who, it was recorded, had died sixteen years earlier after the appearance of the same omen.

The first three deaths occurred in 1635. But an odd fact is that this memorial stone has never been traced. It is not in South Tawton church where there are other tablets to various Oxenhams, nor in any other Devon church or churchyard. So what happened to it, if it really existed, is an additional mystery. It has been suggested that first the Civil Wars intervened, and that later the stone-cutters workshop and its contents might have been destroyed by the Great Fire of London, and so the marble never reached its intended destination.

There is some confusion in old accounts as to whether the marble was intended for South Tawton or Zeal Monachorum, where Oxenhams were also living at this date, But in neither church is there any evidence of this remarkable stone's existence.

About a hundred years later, William Oxenham was living on

a neighbouring farm, Cesslands. As he lay ill one day, he saw the omen in his bedroom. Laughingly he exclaimed that the bird was going to be cheated this time, as he was certainly not "sick unto death". Three days later he was dead, and his name and date are recorded on a tablet in South Tawton church, but with no mention of the White Bird. Nor is there on any of the other family memorials there.

Then there was Margaret Oxenham, usually but erroneously known as Lady Margaret, who was to be married to one of two suitors. On the wedding eve, during a feast given at her home, Oxenham Manor, her father was suddenly aware of the fatal White Bird hovering above his daughter's head, although nobody else saw it. Next day, as she stood with her bridegroom before the altar in South Tawton church, the rejected suitor, dagger in hand, dashed up the aisle and stabbed first Margaret, then himself. One of the rooms in Oxenham Manor is still known as Lady Margaret's Room. One wonders whether Blackmore knew and made use of this Oxenham superstition when writing *Lorna Doone*, in which he incorporates a similar incident.

There are subsequent and rather confused accounts of later manifestations. The omen was seen at the Sidmouth home of an Oxenham, early in the nineteenth century, and—further proof that the bird made good use of its wings—at Kensington in 1873. Here, workmen erecting scaffolding on a house opposite that where a sick Oxenham lay, watched a white bird, which they took to be a dove or pigeon, apparently making repeated attempts to enter a bedroom window. Shortly afterwards that invalid member of the family was dead.

As far as I know, that is the last *recorded* instance of the White Bird's appearance but I am able to bring the story into the present century.

Just before the First World War, friends of ours were living in Barnfield Crescent, Exeter. Their nextdoor neighbour was Amyas Oxenham who died during this period. It was alleged that immediately preceding this event, a white dove flew through his bedroom window, alighting on the writing desk just inside. Here one calls to mind the numerous "cathedral" pigeons of all colours, shapes and sizes that haunt the city. Nevertheless, even if one of them represented the omen in this case, it was a remarkable coincidence conforming to this very old tradition.

Amyas's son, the last of the Oxenhams, died in Canada not long ago, the family being now extinct. History does not relate whether the White Bird followed him across the Atlantic never to return, or whether it was left behind in England with no Oxenhams to haunt. It seems probable, however, that this tradition, curiously persistent for more than three centuries in a small Dartmoor village, has now died with the last member of the family to which it was attached. Certainly none of the later or present occupants of Oxenham Manor have been troubled by the visitations of the White Bird, but then they are not even remotely connected to the Oxenhams, the manor having passed out of the hands of that family in the eighteenth century.

Whatever lies at the root of this superstition, the whole story presents a fascinating, as well as an insoluble mystery. Had the omen been seen only by a dying person, its appearance might have been attributed to the disordered imagination of the sick, aware of the family phantom. But throughout these old records, the various manifestations are vouched for—often on oath—by many seemingly reliable witnesses—nurses, clergy, doctors, attendants and visitors, besides members of the family. Indeed, following the death of the first young John Oxenham mentioned on the missing marble, two attendants who testified to having seen the bird, were carefully examined by order of the Bishop of Exeter. Subsequently two women, present at the death of John's wife, were also officially questioned and since then there have been other interrogations, showing that the matter aroused wide-spread interest and was taken seriously at the time. It is certainly strange that evidence in support of the phantom should have been provided by so many different people from all walks of life, some of whom must surely have been reputable. Yet unless the whole story can be attributed to mass hallucination extending over three centuries, it remains as inexplicable now as in the reign of Charles I.

Baring Gould has suggested that the apparition was equivalent to the "corpse candle", the little blue flame that danced from the churchyard to escort the spirit of a dying person to the tomb of his ancestors. That, however, does not explain the many vouched-for manifestations, both at the manor itself and as far away from the ancestral tomb as South Kensington—a very long "conducted tour".

It has occurred to me, however, that the origin of the haunting might possibly be attributed to a real bird. Oxenham Manor stands in an isolated situation surrounded by narrow lanes, rough copses and marshy fields. Just below the house flows the Oxenham Brook, spanned by a picturesque little stone bridge beneath which dippers often nest. A dipper with its conspicuous white bib, accidentally finding its way into a sickroom, may possibly have been the progenitor, not only of the present day dippers which now confine their hauntings to the stream, but also of the famous White Bird itself. An idea, but again, one which elucidates nothing in the way of solving the mystery.

Birds have always figured conspicuously in omenry, from the times of Roman augury and before, down to the present day, hence, of course the common expression "a bird of ill-omen" Ravens, magpies, even the affectionately-regarded robin, all figure at times in this capacity.

Among countryfolk, the green woodpecker, dubbed the "rain-bird", is still regarded as prophetic, but nowadays of nothing worse than bad weather. A few days ago a young woman assured me that it would shortly rain (a fairly safe forecast this spring) as she had heard the "rain-bird crying" for several mornings. Actually, at this season when all birds are "crying and calling", the green woodpecker's voice has no more significance than that of any other bird. Yet it alone is specially selected from the avian chorus as being of special import. In the green woodpecker's continued role of prophet, we have, I believe, a remnant of really ancient lore.

In Greek mythology, the young man Picus, a rejected suitor of the goddess Pomona, angered the gods by usurping their prerogative in uttering continuous loud-voiced prophecies. By way of terminating this annoyance, Circe, the enchantress, transformed him into a green woodpecker, condemning him to retain the loud voice with which he continues to prophecy innocuously among Pomona's orchard and woodland trees. Ornithologists had this legend in mind when bestowing the generic name *Picinae* upon the woodpecker family.

Greece is a long way from Dartmoor, yet the old belief still flourishes in more modern guise. There being little else of local import to prognosticate in these days, Picus, the green woodpecker, now functions merely as a bad-weather forecaster, the "rain-bird".

As I write, his prophetic voice from the wooded hillside opposite the house, is loudly proclaiming *wet-wet-wet*.

And it is raining.

CHAPTER TWELVE

The Legend of Chaw Gully

No more complete contrast could be imagined than that between the phantom White Bird of Oxenham and the solid, black reality of Dartmoor's raven, both in their respective ways birds of ill-omen associated with death and disaster. The great ebony raven with his uncanny premonition of potential carrion is obviously cast as a harbinger of evil. A cultured and scholarly clergyman of the old-fashioned type, used to say that he felt genuinely perturbed whenever he heard a raven in flight, croaking its way over his rectory. He instinctively considered it a warning of impending death in his parish.

This man was an ornithologist, but apart from others like him and a few moorland farmers, few country folk today can distinguish between crow and raven—or even rook. Old superstitions connected with the bird, have therefore died with lack of recognition. Yet the raven is undoubtedly Dartmoor's own bird, epitomizing its wildness, grandeur and beauty. It might indeed have been chosen for the National Park emblem in place of the anaemic-looking white circus pony which, by no stretch of the imagination, could be said to represent the true Dartmoor breed. By contrast, the raven is grim and forbidding like the terrain he frequents for obvious reasons. Not for nothing has nature endowed him with his great pick-axe beak. Perched on the tors he keeps keen watch, not over buried treasure as related in the legend of Chaw Gully, but for the unburied carcases of the sheep and cattle that strew the hillsides every winter and early spring, particularly after prolonged and severe cold such as was experienced in early 1963. Where the carcase is there will the ravens be gathered together on Dartmoor.

One vivid personal memory of the raven appearing as the very personification of wild Dartmoor remains with me. The date, appropriately enough, was one Hallowe'en when we had walked out to Blacktor, crowned with its triple rock piles. From these rocks we looked down on Blacktor Beare, one of Dartmoor's three curious little oak-copses, clambering up through the moss-covered boulders towards us.

It was a typical late October day, shafts of intense sunshine alternating with heavy purple-black cloud banks that rolled in from the distant coast and emptied themselves upon us in torrential bursts. Sheltering from one such innundation under a ledge of the tor, we watched the rain sweep up the narrow gorge below us and over the tops of the distorted trees, their brown, dry leaves rustling in the storm-wind. Suddenly the rain ceased; dazzling sunlight pierced the clouds, and a brilliant double-rainbow spanned the valley. Crossing that rainbow, his sable plumage irridiscent with its colours, slowly flapped a raven. His entrance can only be described as dramatic. At that moment he seemed to embody the spirit of Dartmoor and to speak with its voice as he *cronk-cronked* hoarsely up the valley passing out of our sight. An insignificant incident, but a clear-cut cameo-memory that remains.

In some similar manner, perhaps, the raven managed to impress its personality upon bygone generations of the "old men", a Dartmoor expression referring exclusively to the former tin-miners. For the bird figures in a rather grim piece of folklore attached to Chaw Gully Mine.

There are two schools of thought as to the probable date of Dartmoor's oldest tin workings. Pros and cons cannot be discussed here, but some authorities consider the trade to have been a going concern in prehistoric times, developing side by side with the Cornish tin industry. There being no *proof* of this, however, others prefer to consider it a medieval development. Detailed records exist showing that mining was flourish-

ing during the reign of King John and his successors. Whatever
its date of origin, Dartmoor tin has been worked and reworked
by successive generations up to the beginning of the present
century. As tools developed from antler or stone pick to miner's
shovel and turbine engine so the workings gradually deepened
from mere surface scratchings to underground adits and
shafts.

Opposite the famous Warren House Inn, the valley and
hillsides are scarred in every direction by gullies, shafts and
spoil heaps, remnants of three of the latest mines to have been
re-opened—Vitifer, Birch Tor, and Golden Dagger. There are
still a few old men left today who worked there as youths.

On the slope of Challacombe Down above, is the deep gash
of Chaw Gully, referred to by these old men as the Roman
Mine. Now the Romans, as far as is known, never exploited the
Dartmoor tin, nor, like the ubiquitous Druids so beloved by an
earlier generation, did they ever set foot up there. How then
has Chaw Gully acquired this local designation? It is an interesting speculation, to my mind indicative of antiquity. Chaw
Gully had probably been worked and re-worked from time
immemorial, and the oldest period with which later miners
might have been familiar from school books, was the Roman.
Among the tinners themselves, therefore, the ancient workings
were dubbed "Roman", simply as a recognition of age.

Its official name Chaw Gully, as printed on maps, is a corruption of Chough. Not that the red-legged, red-beaked Cornish
bird ever inhabited Dartmoor, but "chough" was the old name
for jackdaw. Jackdaws abound here on the steep crags, below
which shafts of considerable depth, now fenced against cattle,
were sunk during later mining operations.

The tin-bearing lodes also produce very small amounts of
gold and, according to tradition, the finest tin and the largest
amounts of gold lie hidden in the depths of Chaw Gully mine.
But they can never be won, for a monster lurks at the bottom
guarding the secret treasure. Perched on the high crag above,
acting as watch-dog, is a fierce old raven—so old, in fact, that

he is reputed to be the very raven that Noah despatched from the Ark.

From time to time, intrepid miners, in search of the hidden mineral wealth, have been lowered down the deep shaft on a rope. Then the raven utters a few hoarse warning croaks, and those watching see a hand holding a knife stretch out from the side of the shaft. It cuts the rope and down crashes the man into the haunted depths. Next morning, his body will be found laid out on the heather above, because the evil spirits dwelling below cannot rest as long as the body of a Christian lies among them.

This belief in a subnormal race of small malevolent human-like beings, living underground, working and jealously guarding the mineral treasure, is very old. They are the Kobbolds of German folk-tales, the Nibelungs of the Rhineland, the Scandinavian trolls, while in stories of Chaldean magic, mineral wealth was guarded by underground demons. Milton alludes to them in *Comus* when he speaks of: "the Goblin or swart fairy of the Mine". On Dartmoor they were known as the "Knockers" because at night, after the legitimate miners had left work, these beings might be heard "knocking", or doing a little mining on their own account. Folklore's continuity provides us with an echo of this old belief in the idea that some vague malignant influence still persists in certain places on the moor today.

As already mentioned, there are people who say frankly that they feel uneasy when on Dartmoor. While appreciating its austere beauty, solitude and peace, they are, at times, oppressed, even briefly overcome, by what one person described to me as a *sense* "not so much of *evil* as of *primeval* forces". They are apt to experience the same kind of unreasoning panic as did the lady on the haunted bridge whose reactions have already been related. *Panic* is the appropriate word, for it is derived simply from Pan, epitomizing natural forces, a sense of whose power overwhelms everyone at times.

One man who frequently walks on the moor says he *never*

looks round as he always has the sensation of being followed. This reaction brings to mind the lines in Coleridge's *Ancient Mariner*:

> Like one that on a lonesome road
> Doth walk in fear and dread,
> And having once turned round, walks on
> And turns no more his head
> Because he knows some fearsome fiend
> Doth close behind him tread.

The vicar of one of our moorland parishes described to me a very odd experience of his own. When seeking relaxation on his rare free days, he was in the habit of taking sandwiches and spending several hours walking on Dartmoor. On this particular occasion he was crossing an insignificant little hollow, indistinguishable from many another, apart from the fact that it was completely enclosed by heather banks, obscuring any view. Suddenly he felt himself to be in an inexplicable manner overwhelmed and, as it were, surrounded by what he described as "all the forces of evil". And, to repeat his own words: "It was only by singing the divine praises that I was enabled to get away from that spot." The rest of his walk was as uneventful as usual, and he added that never before or since had he been through such a spiritual harrowing, either on Dartmoor, or elsewhere.

The vicinity of old mine workings and the stone circles, appear to engender a peculiar aura. Horses especially seem allergic to, and evince keen dislike of some of these places. I know several riders who cannot get their horses through Scorhill Circle, for example. Another friend's mount regularly shied and tried to bolt at the same spot upon an innocuous-looking track skirting the edge of an old tin-working. It is, of course, notorious, that horses are extraordinarily sensitive to, and terrified of the smell of blood. Bloody deeds were undoubtedly perpetrated among the wild and barbarous tinning fraternity of bygone years. Earlier still the stone circles, as mentioned previously, were in all probability scenes of rough justice, perhaps even of sacrifice and ritual murder. To suggest that the "smell of blood" has persisted in such places for centuries is, of course, absurd, but is it possible that certain emanations are liberated in such places, following violence and bloodshed? Science may one day find the solution to such speculations, possibly based on the claim that materialization can take place from freshly-spilled blood. After all, looked upon as it were in reverse, nothing would have appeared more "spooky" and uncanny to the ancient inhabitants of Dartmoor, than present day electricity, wireless and television, with voices and figures taking shape before them as though from the air. Another spot where the remembrance of many evil deeds perpetrated in its prison still lingers is Lydford Castle. In Henry VIII's reign it was described as "one of the most hainous, contagious and detestable places in the realm". Some of this "contagion", it seems, still pervades the ruins. Last year I heard of a teacher who, while being shown round the castle with a party of school children, was so overcome by a sense of horror and evil, that she had to push her way through the crowd of sightseers and escape.

Great Hound Tor, upon the very verge of a road frequented by summer traffic and motor-coaches, has a reputation for eeriness. I have heard this from several separate sources.

"I am a Dartmoor enthusiast," said a lady to me, only a few weeks ago, "but I *cannot* walk upon Hound Tor, or anywhere near it." When I inquired the reason her answer was what one has learned to expect: "I don't know, I can't describe it. I just feel that there is 'something' there, so I avoid that part of the moor." Nor does she feel at ease in the vicinity of Warren House Inn, a place surrounded by derelict mines. She went on to assure me that apart from these two areas she remains completely unaffected and happy everywhere else on Dartmoor.

From at least two independent sources, I have heard an extraordinary tale, with slight variations, about this allegedly haunted tor.

Some years ago, but in the present century, a doctor took a stroll up the short slope of Great Hound Tor, leaving his wife waiting in the car on the road below. When he returned, he appeared to be in a kind of trance, which persisted for forty-eight hours. During this period he muttered in a strange foreign language recognized by a linguist friend as *Hebrew*. Inquiring of one narrator, "Why Hebrew?" I received the reply: "Because the *Egyptians* were once on Dartmoor." This takes some working out, and as far as I know nobody else has been so curiously affected in this particular way upon Hound Tor. The only suggestion I can offer is that the doctor must have encountered the spirit of a wandering Jew, rather than an "Egyptian", one of those workers imported for their inventiveness and ability during the medieval mining boom.

In emitting some indefinable atmosphere or aura which affects certain people adversely, Hound Tor seems to share something in common with the vicinity of Archerton, described in Chapter 14. Both places have been the scenes of former settlements where much human activity must have taken place, and much human emotion been expended. There are Bronze Age kistvaens and other remains in each area, while recent excavations, on Hound Tor, have uncovered the foundations of later dwellings, thought to date from the time of the Conquest or earlier.

* See Postscript, *Sheeps Tor*, p. 190.

CHAPTER THIRTEEN

Jay and Jan

BESIDE the road that runs below Great Hound Tor, between Swine Down and Heatree Cross, lies the pathetic little mound known as Jay's or often incorrectly, Jane's Grave.

Apart from Widecombe and Princetown Prison, this wayside grave outside the Hedge Barton enclosures, evokes more popular interest than any other spot on Dartmoor. Tourist coaches are halted here while their occupants listen open-eyed and -mouthed to the driver-cum-guide relating his own version of this present-day "mystery". For here is a piece of folklore in process of development.

"Notice the flowers on this grave," chants the guide. "They are always fresh, and nobody knows how they get there. It is a mystery." The tourists, suitably impressed and having clicked their cameras, climb back into their seats, and the coach chugs on to Widecombe and Uncle Tom Cobleigh.

Kitty Jay was a poor-house orphan of the nineteenth century. According to custom she was, at an early age, apprenticed as general drudge on a farm at Manaton where, when she was about sixteen years old, she was seduced by a young farm-labourer. Relentlessly persecuted by her employers when her plight became obvious, the miserable girl finally went out and hung herself in one of the barns. As a suicide, she was denied burial in any of the neighbouring churchyards, and so was interred at this wayside spot upon the edge of the moor where the three parishes of Manaton, North Bovey and Widecombe meet, a means of ensuring that none of them claimed any responsibility.

After the lapse of a century, facts had become blurred and

it was rumoured that the grave contained no human, but only "some old sheep" that had died on the moor. (A most unlikely contingency as such corpses are merely left lying on the hillsides for foxes and ravens to clear, or pushed into the nearest stream.) About 1860, James Bryant, then owner of Hedge Barton, determined to ascertain the truth by having the grave excavated. Inside were found a skull and bones, pronounced by pathologists to be those of "a young female person". Bryant had the remains placed in a wooden box, re-interred on the same spot and the little mound raised above, as it is today.

That is the more or less authentic story as far it can be pieced together a century and a half later. But what of the fresh flowers placed upon the grave by unknown hands, constituting today's mystery? For years, the glass jam-jar which remains a permanency on the mound has been, and continues to be, re-plenished with simple nosegays according to season. Primroses, daffodils, bluebells, forget-me-nots, wild marguerites and honey-suckle, a few rhododendron blooms plucked from over the wall of Hedge Barton, or heather from the bank opposite. At Christmas the jar contains holly and evergreens. Whose hands are responsible?

Beatrice Chase, living in her little cottage at nearby Wide-combe and constantly walking the moorland ways, loved a touch of mystery. She it was who, during her lifetime, was unobtrusively responsible, directly or indirectly, for the appearance of these nosegays, while enjoying and propagating the little mystery she thus created. Now she, too, rests in a Dartmoor grave, but still the jam-jar on the mound displays its seasonal flowers and foliage. Perhaps some nearby friend or neighbour continues the kind office where Beatrice left off, touched by the lonely little grave. Tourists and passers-by often add a tribute gathered from the adjoining moor or hedge. However achieved, there is no doubt that the mysterious flowers on Jay's grave are in process of becoming absorbed into Dartmoor's folklore.

As regards myself, these flowers have become a source of

mild amusement. After a lecture, when questions are invited, the first inevitable and even if the *only* query is: "Can you tell us anything about the flowers on Jay's grave?"

As already remarked in the first chapter, Dartmoor legends are, in the main, stern and gloomy, in keeping with their country of origin. Here, by way of contrast, is one of the few in rather lighter vein, the tale of Widecombe Jan. It might perhaps, be called the "inside story" of the great thunderstorm that damaged Widecombe Parish church on Sunday, 21 October 1638. The magnificent tower, sometimes compared to that of Magdalen College, Oxford, was struck by lightning, four people were killed and about sixty injured. An official account of the tragedy may be read in the commemorative verses, written at the time by the village schoolmaster, copies of which hang just inside the tower doorway. The completely *un*official account is as follows:

At that time there lived in Widecombe a bad character named Jan. Having spent all his substance in riotous living, particularly gambling, he sold his soul to the Devil. The bargain was that the Devil handed over some cash then and there for Jan to be going on with but the soul was to be called for later at a more convenient moment. That moment happened to be this fateful Sunday afternoon.

A significant circumstance—recalled afterwards—was that earlier on that same day, a mysterious stranger had visited a local inn. The drink he ordered audibly *sizzled* as he swallowed it, and steam was noticed issuing from his mouth. No wonder that a child, asked in Sunday School to define his "ghostly" enemy replied: "Please, sir, it's the devil, and he du live tu Widecombe."

But to return to Jan. He, hoping to inveigle someone into playing cards with him after service, had crept into a back pew, where he was fast asleep, clutching a pack of cards, "at the ready" so to speak. Suddenly there was a terrific clap of thunder, accompanied by the flash of lightning that struck the tower. The Devil had arrived to complete the bargain and collect Jan's soul. He appeared beside the unsuspecting and bemused sinner, seized him by the collar, and in the general confusion hauled him up to the top of the tower, where the satanic coal-black steed was tethered to one of the pinnacles. Jan, kicking and struggling was hoisted on to its back, the Devil mounting behind. In the take-off, the horse, lashing out with its hoof, kicked off one of the pinnacles—afterwards generally supposed to have been struck by lightning—and away they went through the storm clouds.

As they passed over the Vitifer and Birch Tor valley the still protesting Jan dropped some of the cards that he was still clutching. The four aces were scattered on the hillside below and there one can see them today, turned into four small "intakes" or field enclosures, each shaped like one of the aces. Looking across at them from Warren Inn in the Chaw Gully direction, these little intakes, carved out of the rough moorland, certainly do seem to have been shaped with intent into these playing-card symbols. Particularly clear is that of the ace of diamonds away to the left on the lower slopes of Birch Tor. Each year, however, the resemblance becomes less marked, as the enclosing dry stone walls crumble a little farther to admit the ever-encroaching heath.*

That is the traditional origin of the Ace Fields. One would like to know the actual facts. What prompted some native individualist to carve these tiny oases out of the surrounding wilderness in such unusual form? Four brothers might perhaps have hit upon this novel idea as a means of identification each for his own hard-won plot. But legitimate history is silent on this point, so Widecombe Jan's adventure must serve the purpose. As a wise old moorman, quoted by Val Doone in *We See Devon*, said: "You can't leave the bogs out of Dartymoor, nor the devil, nor the weather, they'm everywheres."

After which, the devil and the weather both having made their appearance in this chapter, here to complete the triumvirate is a purely apocryphal "bog" story.

* See Postcript, *Ace Fields*, p.191

Raybarrow Mire also known as Raybarrow Pool lies on the west slope of Cosdon Beacon being, after Fox-Tor Mires, the most dangerous bog on Dartmoor. In this connection, the word "pool" is even more of a misnomer than when applied to Cranmere. Raybarrow is an extensive area dotted with treacherous green moss-hags, the "stables" holding the bones of many cattle, sheep and ponies. In between, dark pools of water shimmer among patches of rushes and deceptively firm-looking tufts of heather. A rough track, consisting largely of long stretches of brown peaty water, skirts the edge of the bog, but attempts no crossing.

One day a moorman walking along this path spied a hat lying on the surface of the marsh just below him. Stepping cautiously on a few convenient dry tufts, he lifted it up, and to his surprise found a man's head underneath.

"What be you doin' there?" he asked.

"Sitting on me 'oss," came the muffled reply.

Here the intriguing story ends. But, again, like the tale of "salting down feyther", it has a foundation in grim fact, and also points a moral to foolish moor-goers, who refuse to be guided by local knowledge.

The actual tale is, of course, a little piece of absurdity. But the following incident, which I well remember, is not.

Only a few years ago, a young lady from an "up-country" pack (to use a local expression) came out for a day's moorland hunting with the Mid-Devon Hounds. For the occasion she was mounted by the master upon a valuable hunter, and being unfamiliar with this type of country was advised to follow a local lead. She took her own line, however, and before long her mount was floundering in a bog. Soon it was completely "stogged" in a liquid, sucking peat, sinking lower and lower. No help was at hand, but fortunately the girl managed to scramble to safety leaving her horse irretrievably locked in a "Dartmoor stable".

There were two similar occurrences in 1965, the hunter in each case being only just rescued in time.

CHAPTER FOURTEEN

The Hairy Hands

WE now come to one of the most interesting of the Dartmoor stories, being, like the mysterious flowers on Jay's Grave, a product of this century, yet another example of folklore in the making. As far as I have been able to ascertain, there is no mention or hint of the Hairy Hands before the second decade of the present century.

About this period, along a stretch of entirely innocuous-looking road between Postbridge and Two Bridges, a series of unacountable accidents occurred in the neighbourhood of Archerton. Ponytraps overturned into the ditch, cyclists felt their handlebars suddenly wrenched out of control and their machines, mounting the grass verge, crashed into the stone wall. Horses shied, bolted and threw their riders. Cars and motor-coaches skidded, sometimes with fatal results. A doctor from Princetown was riding his motor-cycle with two children in the sidecar, when the whole engine detached itself without warning. Although the children were thrown clear, the man was killed. The climax to these incidents was reached shortly afterwards, when a young Army officer was injured in a crash on his motor-cycle. He afterwards described how, a second before the impact, he had been distinctly aware of a pair of large muscular, hairy hands that closed over his own, forcing his machine off the road.

Widespread attention now became focused upon this piece of roadway, and publicity was unleashed. The *Daily Mail* got hold of the story in the autumn of 1921 and sent down reporters to investigate.

HAIRY HANDS ON DARTMOOR

became sensational front page news overnight. Publicity reached such a pitch that eventually the road authorities were called in to carry out a thorough investigation. As a result, the camber on that stretch of road was declared to be at fault; repairs were put in hand, and that for a time was considered by the more level-headed to be the practical answer to the sinister riddle, the Hairy Hands themselves being dismissed as a piece of imaginative journalese.

About three years later, however, a woman with her husband was sleeping in a caravan near the same spot. Subsequently she published an account of how, one bright moonlight night, she woke to see a large hairy hand clawing up and down the window, beneath which her husband lay asleep. Sensing that evil was threatening him she slipped from the bunk on to her knees and made the sign of the cross, whereupon "The Hand" vanished. Although she never saw it again, she confessed to a curious sensation of *malaise* when in the vicinity, and afterwards deliberately avoided that part of the moor.

Since these two appearances there is no record, as far as I know, of the Hairy Hands having actually been seen again. Yet undoubtedly, a sneaking belief persists that their—or some other undefined—sinister influence still pervades that area today.

Four years ago I was told of a young man driving from Plymouth to Chagford one evening. He never arrived at his destination but was found dead near this same spot underneath his overturned car. Expert examination of both the body and the car, so my informant averred, could arrive at no satisfactory conclusion to account for either death or accident. More recently there have been vague rumours of renewed activity by the hands—or those of a counterpart—nearer to Princetown, in the vicinity of Rundlestone, but there seem to be no confirmatory details.

In 1958 a woman I met told me of a curious experience she

had while staying near Archerton only a short time before. She described how, one afternoon, she went for a stroll through the surrounding rough enclosures. As she was walking through one of the plantations she became, without warning, another of these victims of sudden inexplicable panic, accompanied by a sensation of being "rooted to the spot and unable to move". Summoning all her will-power she at length started to run, as she put it, "in an absolute blind funk", slipped, and fell into the leat that flows through the wood. This unexpected cold douche apparently broke the spell, and coming to, she returned home without further trouble. But like the lady in the caravan, she insisted that nothing would induce her to walk on that part of the moor again alone.

Other instances and oblique references to these Hairy Hands crop up from time to time, demonstrating that a new twentieth-century superstition seems to be gradually building up along this particular Dartmoor road. Reactions to these accounts, of course, vary. By most people they are, as might be expected, contemptuously dismissed as arrant nonsense, although all evince interest. Others rather uncertainly, think that there "may be something in it". A minority, presumably of the more psychic type, express belief in the presence of an indefinite malignant influence. To what exactly this is to be attributed, or what constitutes the nature of the indefinable sensations undoubtedly experienced by certain individuals in certain places, there is no answer at present.

One suggestion advanced is that they emanate from, and are indicative of the vague beings—if one can so designate something that has no actual being—generally classed as elementals. Elementals may loosely be described as disembodied matter, neither of the human nor of the spirit world, but earthbound between the two. They are nebulous and semi-formless, any semblance they may have approaching that of an ape, hence, possibly, the "hairiness" of the hands. Elementals are, in fact, an unfinished product, still largely "null and void". In this unhappy state they engender an indefinable aura of malaise, powerful enough at times to penetrate into the everyday world where its presence may be felt by certain sensitive individuals.

Another slant on the elemental portrays it as an earth-bound spirit, freed from the body but not from the scene of some crime committed during life. A third theory is that both panic-fear and Hairy Hands are caused by thought-materialization, or by what might perhaps be described as *violence*-materialization. It is significant that in practically every case, these peculiar sensations are experienced in places which, in all probability, were the former scenes of violent deeds and emotions, such as the stone circles and tin mines. The spot where the reputed Hairy Hands manifest themselves, for instance, was, like Hound Tor in prehistoric times, a thickly populated area, and remains of the Bronze Age burial kists are still to be seen there today.

In *My Occult Case Book*, Frank Lind describes similar hauntings thus: "It seems probable that they are in the nature of imprints on the ether, left there by powerful psychic vibrations, set in motion by some violent or tragic event and recurring at intervals. These intervals are likely to have a longer and longer gap between them similar to the widening circles caused by a stone thrown into smooth water."

This raises the question whether intense emotion either of primitive or modern origin can be concentrated with such force as to form definite emanations, which brings us back again to the ectoplasmic theory of freshly-shed blood, mentioned in a previous chapter. Can such materialization be considered any more incongruous than, as already suggested, the appearance of a television personality would have been to a prehistoric man, had such a vision suddenly materialized before him out of a box—or in his case, from a stone chest?

In the same way, much that seems inexplicable and uncanny at present, will almost certainly receive rational explanation, according to natural laws, by future scientists. Meanwhile everyone may freely indulge in his own speculations.

By way of postscript, it is interesting to compare the Dartmoor Hairy Hands with a somewhat similar superstition, prevalent not so long ago in the Colebrook district, near Crediton. Here, in a certain lane, a creature described as "looking something like a red monkey" would jump out upon a passer-by, following him as far as the village, when it would disappear. Perhaps another manifestation of a hairy elemental.

By way of pleasant contrast to these sinister tales, is a recent and entirely novel sequel. One has, so to speak, lived with the Hairy Hands for many years, but not until a few months ago had I ever heard of what may be described as a Benevolent Hand. I record its entry with pleasure, but without comment, just as the story was told to me by a man who is a great lover of, and a great walker upon Dartmoor. Oddly enough, in spite of his extensive knowledge of the moorland ways, he had never succeeded in locating the Phillpotts Cuttings, familiar to all moormen and hunting people.

When Frank Phillpotts hunted the Mid-Devon Hounds at the turn of the century, in order to facilitate passage through the deep, tortuous peat veins of the great northern bog, he instigated the cutting of certain paths. They were formed by paring away the peat down to solid granite level, the route being marked by little cairns of white stone with the later addition, after his death, of commemorating plaques. This was a far-sighted and colossal task, the results proving of the greatest benefit to cattle-drivers, walkers, huntsmen and hounds. Anyone who has tried to find a way through this baffling maze of deep peat fissures sometimes so high that they obscure the view together with any sense of direction, realizes what a boon these crossing-places are. One white-cairned cutting gives access through the Hangingstone Hill area, this being the particular cutting that my narrator had sought many times in vain.

One day, early in 1964, after yet another unsuccessful search, feeling thoroughly irritated by repeated failure, he threw down the thumb-stick he always carries, sat on a stone and lit a cigarette. As he rested there, he noticed that his stick was beginning to revolve slowly, entirely of its own volition, until its handle was in front of him "waiting to be picked up". Responding to the invitation, at the same moment he became conscious of the firm yet gentle grasp of a hand upon his wrist, as though urging him forward. Picking up his stick, he rose, allowing the invisible hand to lead him. Guided thus, in a few moments he found himself looking at the long-sought cairn indicating the Phillpotts Cutting.

That is the story as it was told to me. Apropos of the revolving stick, I will only add an experience of my own. One day four of us set out by a rather circuitous and unfamiliar route from Shipley Bridge on the Avon to reach Erme Pound. It was a fine summer day, but before we were anywhere near our objective, thunderclouds rolled up, torrential rain descended and all landmarks were obliterated in thick mist. Becoming uncertain of our bearings, we took out a compass, steadied it on a rock and crouched over it. The pointer moved slowly, then faster, finally spinning rapidly round and round like a teetotum. The sight was so absurd that we were reduced to helpless laughter, then, having pulled ourselves together trudged on. In the opaque gloom we overshot our target by about three miles, finally regaining our starting point wet through. The dense steam engendered by four sodden people, plus two sodden dogs, eventually shut inside a small car, rivalled the mist outside on the moor. But what "got" that compass remains a minor mystery.

Twice only in many years of Dartmoor walking, have I myself been conscious of slight uneasiness. Each time this happened upon Great Lynx or Lynch Tor, one of Dartmoor's grandest piles, overlooking the Lyd valley. Upon the slope, between the river and the tor lies the scattered evidence of old tin-workings, together with the ring-foundations of prehistoric dwellings.

I have crouched under the massive rocks of Great Lynx with four companions when a raging gale swept away every word as soon as uttered, making the briefest communication virtually impossible. Again, up there with my husband one day, we were, almost without warning, suddenly enveloped in a typical Dartmoor mist. Thick, opaque and silently obliterating, it created a curious sense of other-worldliness, an isolation in time, and severance from all normal contacts. Fear lurked hidden in the mist wraiths, and had one been alone might have leaped out and taken control.

Upon another occasion, leaving two companions sheltering under the lee-side of the rock-pile, I picked an arduous way through the scarred and desolate peat veins that stretch between Great Lynx and that tall ruinous building, well named Bleak House, upon the banks of the little Rattle Brook. Perched high on a ledge that once supported floor-boards, long since rotted, was the nest of a raven, fitting tenant for such a place. Outside, half-engulfed in the surrounding morass, old pieces of rusty metal, together with rounded humps of boilers from the abandoned peat-enterprise, lay like wallowing, prehistoric corpses. Storm clouds hung in a leaden sky, yet there was a curious stillness, with no wind stirring the reed-patches. The whole atmosphere of the place exuded such chill eeriness that it was a relief to turn back and be linked again to humanity. Whenever I recall that spot on that particular day, it is epitomized in my mind by the Biblical phrase, "the abomination of desolation".

Something to that effect is, I think, the root-cause of Dartmoor's peculiar, and at times uncanny atmosphere. By contrast with the noisy crowded state in which we are now compelled to live, isolation *can* become the abomination of desolation. Familiar as one may be with the moor in all its moods, good and bad, at times there arises an acute consciousness of implacable, unrelenting, natural forces watchfully gathered all round, pressing closer as skies darken, wind sweeps by and rain or mist descends. The effect engendered is one of loneliness, littleness and helplessness, the border-line between an eerie feeling and plain fear being narrower than is sometimes realized.

Val Doone, describing Dartmoor wrote: "The Moor is elemental. The thin veneer of civilization has never been spread over it. Its landscape and weather alike go back to the simple uncompounded elements of the world, stark, natural and lovely."

Some people then, even today, feel that there is more than meets the physical eye on Dartmoor. Few, it seems, experience the beneficial guidance of benevolent phantom hands, although, fortunately, most of us remain unaffected by the extreme mental discomfort that undoubtedly affects others at times. The more we see of the moor, the greater becomes its magnetizm.

CHAPTER FIFTEEN

Witchcraft

FEW things are subject to more popular misconception than witchcraft. In fact current belief on the topic might be said to constitute a modern superstition in itself. The following chapters give some account of the remnants of this ancient cult as they are still to be found in Dartmoor and other Devonshire villages today.

There are many enlightening and fascinating works on witchcraft, from Dr. Margaret Murray's large tome, *The Witch Cult of Western Europe*, to G. B. Gardner's explanatory book, *Witchcraft Today*, and T. C. Lethbridge's erudite little volume entitled quite simply *Witches*. These and other works cover the wide general field, but for the better understanding of the fragments that linger in the West Country today, a brief preliminary explanation is necessary.

There are two popular reactions to witches and their works: (a) they are purely comic characters, embedded in a fairy-tale setting and (b) they are wholly evil characters in league with the Devil. In either case witches are considered to be wicked old women who cast spells and are inextricably mixed up with black cats, high hats, sabbats, broomsticks and bubbling cauldrons of revolting ingredients.

Most popular misconceptions however are based on fact that, like folklore, has become distorted in the course of time. Broomsticks had their origin in fertility poles; high hats were fashionable in medieval times when witchcraft was first pronounced to be a heresy and witch-hunts were inaugurated. As for cats, many a lonely woman kept one for company, the "spinster's cat" being, proverbial. Today, it is more often the

Spinster's Rock, Drewsteignton—the only remaining cromlech in Devon

Dartmoor's grim raven

Dartmoor landmarks: (*left to right*) the Longstone, a tall menhir on Shuggle Down; an incised stone, Stickle-path; Bowerman's Nose, one of Dartmoor's more curious "men"

"spinster's dog", the poodle, the peke, or the spaniel that trots along on its lead beside its mistress on her outings, but the underlying purpose remains the same. Witches were also, in the first instance, the wise women (or men) of their own small community, skilled in the brewing of herbal remedies and simples. The counterpart of the old black cauldron may be seen in many a gipsy encampment today, or in old Dartmoor farmyards where, as "crock" or "skillet", it is filled either with fowl's food, or geraniums, according to taste. We ourselves have one such dilapidated specimen serving as a flowerpot on top of our old stone mounting steps.

The truth is very different from these twisted notions that are so firmly embedded in the popular imagination. *True* witchcraft was, and still is, a religious cult. Our remote ancestors worshipped the personified forces of nature, particularly the sun and moon. The witches' religion has its foundations in a moon-cult with implicit belief in the efficacy of fertility rites. The higher its devotees could leap on their poles (as likely as not an old broomstick, for this was the religion of simple folk) over the sprouting corn, the higher would grow the crops. The more frenzied the dances by moonlight the more beneficent would be the influence exercised by their moon-goddess, Tana, Arianod, Epona, Diana, Astarte, call her what you will. She appears under many different names, in many guises and disguises, in almost every country of the world. According to ancient belief in sympathetic magic, the punctilious practice of these rites was essential to ensure fertility, and thus, continuity of human life, domestic and wild creatures (the food supply) and vegetation.

After the introduction of Christianity into Britain, for several centuries the old and the new religions existed peaceably side by side, with many converts keeping a foot in both camps for safety. One freshly-Christianized king, indeed, was reputed to have erected a Christian altar at one end of his newly-built church, and a pagan sacrificial altar at the other, to be sure of getting the best of both worlds.

In the thirteenth century, the Pope, determined to eliminate the "old religion" once and for all, declared its continued practice to be a heresy after which, like all banned activities, then and now, witchcraft became an underground movement, with its adherents suffering centuries of totally unjustified persecution. Witch-hunting was almost a national sport, thousands of innocent men, women, and even children being burned at the stake. Facts were exaggerated, incidents distorted and trumped up charges brought against any unpopular or eccentric individual; one lasting result of all this being the garbled version of witchcraft as generally accepted today.

The word *witch*, allied to *wit*, is usually considered to be derived from the Anglo-Saxon *wicca*, a witch meaning simply "a wise person", man or woman. Of whichever sex, the witch was often naturally gifted, and trained to use his or her gifts and wits to advantage in accordance with the tenets of the "craft", that being what we should today perhaps call "natural science".

Every village or small community contained one or two such individuals. They studied, noted and could predict natural effects such as weather changes, moon phases, movement of tides and so on. They concocted brews from the plants around them. Those with the requisite gift practised their "healing" arts, as do their descendants today in many a Dartmoor village and town. They had, in fact, much in common with the African tribal witch-doctor, both past and present. Their simpler, uninitiated neighbours inevitably held them in a certain amount of awe, and the witches doubtless upheld their prestige by playing upon credulity when expedient. Belief in their supernatural powers increased as the cult was driven ever further into secrecy. It was argued—quite logically—that if they were really capable of bringing about the beneficient results for which they claimed credit, they must equally well be able to work evil. And so arose that implicit belief in the *power* of witchcraft which is not yet wholly dead.

Here we come to the crux of the matter, and down to fundamentals. All religious beliefs are based on *faith*, and the ability to concentrate will-power. Christians hold that faith "can remove mountains" and perform miracles of healing. Indeed there are revivalist movements to this effect at the present time. On the day that I was writing this chapter (22 February 1964) *The Western Morning News* reported these words from a speech made by the Bishop of Plymouth at a meeting of The Guild of Health: "The sad thing historically is that from very early times, say about A.D. 400 or 500, the Church gradually became separated from scientific healing. We have gone our separate ways. There is a great feeling throughout, among doctors and clergy that we should come and work together again."

An interesting statement.

Christian Science, too, teaches that ills are non-existent, as long as they are banished from the mind. Witches believe that —like the faith that removes mountains—concentration of will-power can bring about physical and mental change. In *The Magic Arts in Britain*, Lewis Spence writes: "According to Witch doctrine, a unity existed in nature . . . its underlying elements were the same and capable of alteration by will-power which could reshape these into any desired form." True witches are trained in this intense concentration, "As I will, so mote it be" being one of their tenets.

It is only reasonable to suppose that this talent—if so it may be called—must work either way. It may be turned to good account, as during the Second World War when the present-day witch societies claim to have stopped Hitler's invasion of England by a combined concentration of will-force. The reverse, evil aspect is evident in the many related instances, real or imaginary, of "ill-wishing", "cursing" and "over-looking". It is only logical to assume that this powerful ability must be applied in *both*, or in *neither* direction.

The question "Do you believe in witches?" is one that is often asked. The answer must be that *of course* one believes in witches because modern witch societies exist as "going concerns" in several parts of the British Isles today, with a total membership of four or five hundred at the time of writing. One might as well ask, "Do you believe in Freemasons, or Mormons or Plymouth Brethren?" All, including witches, are sects having their own tenets, creeds and rituals. It is quite a different matter to query belief in witch-*power*, that is the recognized ability to bring about change for good or evil according to desire. The answer to that question must remain an individual decision.

It is an interesting fact that belief in this type of power has lingered longer in the West Country than anywhere else, due, it is alleged, to the teaching of the Reverend John Wesley who drew his largest followings from Devon and Cornwall. He himself firmly believed in the evil side of this practice, teaching that to deny its existence was to deny Bible truth, for in Exodus, chapter 22, we read the exhortation: "Thou shalt not suffer a witch to live." Doubtless this text, as well as convincing John Wesley, has served as the basis for many a witch-hunt and bitter persecution in the past.

The last witch-burning in England took place at Exeter in the seventeenth century, so possibly it is not surprising that remnants of this once prevalent acceptance of witchcraft's efficacy still lingers in some parts of Devon today.

It cannot however be emphasized too strongly that here it has become completely divorced from any religious background or significance, nor have any of today's witches the slightest connection with modern witch societies, of whose existence they are certainly totally unaware. Our "witches" are ordinary unpretentious folk, usually villagers from the humbler walks of life who happen to be possessed of the mysterious "power", combined with the *natural* ability to make use of it. Certainly they do not consider themselves to be "witches" in the generally accepted sense of the word, though the term is a convenient one, and used here throughout, for lack of a better.

When we talk of witchcraft today on Dartmoor, it denotes two quite different things.

(1) The reputed ability to ill-wish, or curse, or over-look with the evil-eye which is Black Witchcraft.

(2) A genuine and natural gift of healing, "blessing" or "charming" away certain minor ailments, an ability which is the wholly beneficient "White Witchcraft".

Logically, of course, the same person is able to practise both forms of the craft as occasion demands. These half-and-half individuals were once known as "grey" witches, but the term has now fallen into disuse and I have never heard it used.

While nobody owns to being a black practitioner, many towns and almost every village around Dartmoor still have somebody who can act in the capacity of white witch when occasion demands, exercising the ability without either advertisement or secrecy. People seek their services for relief from warts, ring-worm, burns or bleeding on behalf of themselves, their children or domestic animals, visiting the witch as naturally as they would the doctor or vet.

Rather oddly, most of these white witches are men, and most of the black witches, women. The word "wizard" is never heard except in fairy-tales, where the conventional wizard had more the character of a magician than of a true witch. It is indeed unfortunate that the same word "witch" has to be employed to denote both kinds of the craft, good and bad, no other term having been found to define specifically the white witch's beneficial ministrations. Neither "healer", nor "charmer" quite meets the case.

Not long ago I met a woman who described how her "Granny" used to "bless for bleeding". As children she and all the neighbours would run to Granny to have any bad wounds or cuts "blessed" to arrest the bleeding. "But," added her granddaughter, "we never heard the word 'witch' mentioned in connection with Granny who was a *dear* old soul. We should *never* have thought of her as a witch."

That sentiment serves to emphasize the point, and at the same time to demonstrate how inevitably sinister implications are now attached to the word in popular imagination, although formerly this was far from being the case. Nor is it given this interpretation in modern witch societies.

CHAPTER SIXTEEN

Black Witchcraft

THE outstanding point about black witchcraft in Devon today, lies not in its practice, for that is virtually extinct, but in the lingering *belief* that it can still operate. Admittedly this belief in the ability to harm by deliberately "ill-wishing", "cursing" or "over-looking" is rapidly diminishing, but I have come across more genuine instances than would perhaps be readily credited today—outside the West Country. Only this year (1964) a woman assured me in all seriousness of her conviction that a neighbour was guilty of ill-wishing. She—my informant—never passes the suspect's cottage door without making the sign of the cross. Local doctors, up to the present time, have found great difficulty in treating patients belonging to "the old school of thought", convinced that their illnesses had been caused by someone with whom they had quarrelled. Such cases can usually be explained on the "mind over matter" principle, but they pose a problem for the modern medical practitioner.

I have heard of a man being cursed (in the sense of being ill-wished) by a neighbour to the extent of hoping that all his children would be born blind. The husband went home in perturbation and foolishly reported this to his wife who was expecting a child. The baby was born blind. Another obvious case, this time of pre-natal suggestion. At the time however, it was, of course, cited as a positive result of ill-wishing.

Fear of witches and their real or supposed machinations was once very real, as evidenced by the story of the sexton, who, having dug the grave for a reputed witch, was seen, after the funeral service, laboriously turning the coffin upside down before filling in the grave. Asked for an explanation by a puzzled onlooker he replied: "If 'er do get out and start to diggy, 'er can only diggy down'ards."

Reminiscent of the days when any eccentric or unpopular person might, with no justification whatever, be accused of witchcraft, is the following incident. Inevitably, as in all these stories, real names must be withheld, for obvious reasons.

Ten years ago I was being driven to a lecture by a local taximan. As we passed the gateway of a farm, standing on the edge of the open moor, the man asked whether I knew the farmer's wife. I replied that I had met her at Women's Institute meetings, and as a member of the local drama group. She had always appeared pleasant and friendly. "Maybe," said the driver in a significant tone. "But they all have to be very careful. Nobody likes to vote against her." After a little tactful pressure on my part, he embarked upon details.

The farmer's wife had a brother John, also a farmer, with whom she had quarrelled; after which every kind of misfortune beset John. It was the usual story—wife and children ill, cattle dying, crops failing, poultry ceasing to lay, and so on. Convinced eventually that he was being ill-wished by some unknown person, he went to Exeter for consultation with a well-known white witch. This man confirmed his suspicions, and in order to identify his ill-wisher, John was given the following instructions. He was to mount the rough cob which he used for rounding up his sheep on Dartmoor, leave the reins loose, and let the animal go where it pleased. It would stop outside the house of his enemy. John followed instructions, and the horse came to a halt outside his sister's farm—the gate that we had just passed.

Of course, what immediately comes to mind is that previous to the quarrel the horse had probably been more accustomed to stopping there than anywhere else. The interest of this story however, lies not in the extremely doubtful desire or ability on the part of the farmer's wife to ill-wish, but in the fact that several people obviously *believed* that she could and did. Brother John was convinced of it. So apparently was the Exeter white witch, while there was no doubt at all about the taximan's opinion. Also, according to him, some members of the Institute to which, by the way, the perfectly respectable lady still belongs, are not too comfortable about it either.

The white witch mentioned here was an eighty-seven years old man who lived near Ottery St. Mary, and has recently died. For years he regularly attended every Friday market in Exeter in his recognized capacity, advising on tricky problems similar to that of Brother John and, among other accomplishments, "shaking hands for warts"—one of the many methods of cure.

Some of these alleged ill-wishers, if they were cunning enough, enjoyed and did very well out of their doubtful reputations. One such character was Alice, a well known personality in a small town just before the last war. Although few people owned to belief in her craft, most took pains to placate her "just in case", possibly with some justification. She was said to have "over-looked" a man's horses with the result that all the foals were still-born, and the following incidents were related to me by Rose, now a married woman who, as a girl, had reason to remember Alice's activities.

The old lady used to wander round the countryside, acquiring loot, and one day turned up at the farm where Rose lived with her parents. Having announced that she wanted to buy a small pig, she was taken to a sty, where she immediately pointed out the animal she fancied. That particular piglet was refused her, but another offered in its stead. This she angrily rejected and walked off muttering that if *she* couldn't have that pig, nobody else should. Next day that little pig was found dead in the sty.

On another occasion, according to Rose who was in the dairy churning at the time, Alice suddenly appeared at the window and asked for a pound of butter. As the butter was needed for making up next day's market consignment, this request also met with refusal, so she flounced off in a temper. "And," said Rose, "do you know, we just couldn't get that butter to come, and we never did. We had to leave it."

As a general rule, however, most people were only too anxious to placate Alice. A near neighbour of hers described her doorstep as resembling a votive altar, a receptacle for offerings. Fresh eggs, dishes of cream, fruit, vegetables, a bit of pork when someone killed a pig, anything of this sort might be seen lying there. Nor would anyone dare to "pinch" some item before Alice looked out to collect her spoils.

Now this woman was an interesting character and certainly possessed the "wit" to play upon the credulity of her neighbours. Whether, in addition, she really believed herself to be endowed with the ability to make use of the "black power" is another question. A friend, who knew her well, told me that she once visited Alice in hospital to which she had been removed with a serious illness. Screens had been placed round her bed, her reaction to them being the remark: "They've put screens round my bed, but the Devil isn't coming for old Alice yet!" Nor did he. At any rate she recovered and continued to flourish on free-will offerings for several more years.

One cannot help speculating as to exactly *what* she meant by that remark. Was it intended as a grim joke? Was she one of the last of the true black witches who genuinely believed themselves to be in league with the Devil and capable of working harm at pleasure? Or was she, even in her serious plight, still acting a part that had paid her handsomely? The cunning old woman finally took her secrets with her to the grave.

Alice *may* have believed in the Devil; the rector of a small rural parish consisting of a scattered agricultural community certainly did. He assured me that the Devil was then (about seven years ago) active in his village. Black magic and ill-wishing were being resorted to, he said, proof of which was to be seen in significant signs chalked on doorsteps, and traced in the dust or snow outside gateways. From this same country community I also collected accounts of charming by white witches, and more about the fascinating subject of magic circles, some account of the latter being given in the next chapter.

Now my intention in writing these chapters on witchcraft had been to confine myself strictly to incidents of which I have had first-hand experience or knowledge. The following story, however, is so remarkable that it merits inclusion. It is an account of her father's death sent to *The Western Morning News* by Miss Sylvia Calmady-Hamlyn, and published on 25 June 1953, the events she relates having occurred sixty years previously.

Miss Calmady-Hamlyn's name was well-known in Devon and beyond. She was an ardent advocate for and breeder of the true Dartmoor pony, for whose reinstatement she worked untiringly as president of the Dartmoor Pony Club for a number of years. Nobody who ever saw her solid, sturdy figure, tramping in gumboots through the mud of many a pony show would be likely to consider her as given to romancing. Yet she sent this letter to the Press for publication. Here, verbatim, are the relevant extracts from her account, headed:

THREE LIFTON MAGISTRATES DIED—BY WITCHCRAFT?

It came as something of a shock, after sixty years to read the brief account given at the Devonshire Association's meeting in Plymouth of the events involving my father's death in September 1897.

My father . . . was a scholar of Baliol . . . a Prize Essayman and History First, and then barrister at Lincoln's Inn. He also wrote regularly for the *Pall Mall*, the *Spectator* and the *Anti Jacobin*. His interests being in London, he only came to Leawood (the family home) for the three summer months, where his stepmother joined us to keep house.

I was about 10 when we first went there and rode my Dartmoor pony a good deal about the district.

He made me promise never to go on a certain rather poor little farm lying under the Moor . . . He told me once that there were bad people called black witches who did harm to their neighbours but that quite harmless old women often got that reputation, and that he and I were going to take soup to one such victim—living in great poverty and isolation, because the villagers refused to allow her to come to the village. . . .

On September 1st 1897, we rode, as was his custom, to Lifton

Court, the other two magistrates being Mr. Kelly of Kelly and a man whose name I forget.

The noted black witch had been summoned for the first time by the police for some offence of theft, and the magistrates gave her some fine—my father, I think, being in the chair.

As they left the courthouse, she stood on the steps and cursed them giving my father at most three days to live, Mr. Kelly two years, and the third man three years.

Of course Bridestowe village rang that night with the news of the cursing of the magistrates—particularly of "Squire".

On September 2nd he went out riding about 10.30 a.m. while I was still at lessons.

At 12, a frightened tenant came with news of an "accident to Squire" and we waited.

At 3, the Rector came and told us that my father had been found dead, with his horse standing by, at a spot not far from the black witch's holding. He was 44.

Within two years I was visiting my step-grandmother at Exmouth where she lived, and saw a paralysed, helpless man in a bath chair—Mr. Kelly of Kelly, who shortly died.

The third magistrate died within the limit of his curse.

I did not know the story until, at 21, I returned to Bridestowe . . . when the Rector told me, and added: "I have preached against the power of witchcraft all my time, and after that it was no longer any good."

Surely a most remarkable story, which also throws a good many sidelights on witchcraft as regarded at that date. Incidentally the court at Lifton, where these strange happenings were recorded, was closed at the end of November 1960, after functioning for three hundred years.

The next account, is one of the few instances of ill-wishing that I have actually encountered—and that only a year or so ago; and it came of something of a shock to hear such sentiments expressed by an educated woman of good standing, in the twentieth century.

Owner of a certain amount of property, she had fallen out with one of her tenants, and was enumerating the man's misdeed's. She ended the recital by saying, "But I've put the witch's curse on him to pay him out and I know it's working." Naturally I took this as a joke, but she assured me that she was serious. As proof she added that the man's wife had been bedridden for weeks, having been unaccountably laid low by illness. When I expressed the opinion that it was tough luck on the wife, I was informed that the curse extended to the whole family because "they were all in it—as bad as each other." I inquired the nature of the curse but it was not divulged.

Meeting her again some weeks later I jokingly asked how the ill-wishing was progressing, to be told that it was all over. She and the tenant had settled their differences, she had "lifted the curse" and the woman was recovering.

At the time of writing, there are reports in the newspapers of an altercation taking place between a rector and his parishioners. As a result the rector has officially cursed any person who gives information upon parochial affairs to the Press or to his bishop. The latter, on his part, has stated that no ordained minister has authority to indulge in the practice of placing a particular curse on individual people.

One wonders whether there is such a thing as a "holy" or "white" curse, justified by its deliverance in righteous indignation.

CHAPTER SEVENTEEN

More Black Witchcraft

I N the last chapter, mention was made of "grey" witches, those who make use of either the black or white art as circumstances dictate.

Three years ago, water-pipes were being laid through our garden, under the direction of a young, up-to-date silk-shirted foreman, named Bert.

A discussion with him about water-pipes led to the subject of water-divining or "dowsing" and he mentioned that his grandfather, still living in a small Devonshire village, is a recognized dowser. "And," added Bert, "he charms for warts and ring-worm as well." There was nothing particularly unusual about this, but I became more interested when he went on to say, quite casually, that "Granfer" could ill-wish as well and related the following example of his ability in this direction.

Granfer (obviously a talented man, descendant of the true witch breed, well endowed with the old primitive skills) runs a smallholding on which he keeps a few cows. For no apparent reason all his milk became tainted and turned bad. An official called in from the Milk Marketing Board, was unable to find any cause for the trouble. Granfer then bethought him of a reputed witch-woman in the next parish, with whom he was not on the best of terms, and felt convinced that everything could be traced to her as she must have over-looked his cows. He therefore decided to put a counter-curse upon her, which he did, apparently with satisfactory results. "Anyhow," ended Bert, "the milk's been all right ever since." Proof positive.

An interesting sequel followed. As described in Chapter 22 custom decrees that these old healing charms must be passed down alternately from man to woman in each succeeding generation of the family until a member is found with the ability to make use of it. Granfer having no female relative to inherit his wart and ring-worm charms was considering the suitability of Bert's girl-friend, a young lady supervisor from Woolworth's Stores.

The last time I saw Bert, he had arranged to take her out on the back of his motor-bike that same Saturday evening to see Granfer. He assured me that I should hear the result of this momentous interview, but fate intervened, transferring Bert, at a moment's notice, to other spheres.

I have never seen him since, but conclude that the young lady must have failed to reach the required standard, for this reason. Shortly afterwards, an Okehampton woman told me that her daughter, aged ten, had been given a wart-charm by a white witch who, from her description, could have been none other than Granfer. According to her mother, the child has accepted this responsibility in all seriousness, has tried out the charm, but is rigidly observing the essential secrecy enjoined upon her. One would like to know whether Granfer, by some mysterious instinct, was able to recognize the requisite ability dormant in this child, as compared with its presumed absence in the young lady from Woolworths?

It will be interesting to follow the subsequent career of this potential young white witch for it seems highly improbable that many more of them will be turned out from our new schools and universities. I know of one other youngster, however. His mother told me that Richard, aged seven was curing his sister's warts by rubbing them every morning with his "lick".

Richard certainly has the right idea though one wonders where he acquired it. Saliva is used freely in many of the old witchcraft charms—as well as for curses, and this fact invites investigation into its curative properties, from a medical point of view. Christ cured a man's blindness by spitting upon his eyes. Spitting also figured in many of the ancient religious ceremonies of Egypt where the saliva of the gods was held to bestow healing. When Ra, the sun-god, was blinded Thoth restored his sight by spitting in the affected eye. African witch-doctors still cement contracts, friendships and curses by spitting, while stones are spat upon to ensure a safe journey. The latter is an interesting point, for I have heard that among gipsies it was customary to spit upon the milestones that they passed in their caravans, though for what reason I have been unable to discover. A wounded animal invariably licks its sores assiduously, and other instances of this ubiquitous custom might be quoted. Palestine, Africa, the witches and gipsies of the English countryside—a long chain of links yet to be unravelled.

Mr. Bruce Oliver, writing in the *Transactions of the Devonshire Association*, perhaps throws a little light upon the subject when he tells us that witches believe spittle to contain the essence of personality. It would appear, therefore, that by the act of spitting, a certain amount of influence or power is ejected upon a selected spot, which brings us back again to the various methods by which will-power may be concentrated and exerted for good or for evil impartially.

For some years, we had as near neighbour Mary Ann, a village woman reputed to be a witch, black or white according to fancy. Next door to her lived a small tradesman Ben, with whom she was at loggerheads. One day, according to village gossip, she was seen to spit three times upon Ben's doorstep, muttering vindictively: "Take that! Take that! Take that!" Whether coincidence or not, from that time nothing prospered with the man, whom we knew quite well. His wife died, his little business failed, and he became stone deaf, dying in his early fifties. An odd tale of disasters, reminiscent of Miss Calmady-Hamlyn's story.

As already stated, Mary Ann was a "grey" or "double-ways" witch, and could benefit those in her good books. At that time, we had in our service a young girl whose widowed mother and

The White Lady of Lydford Gorge

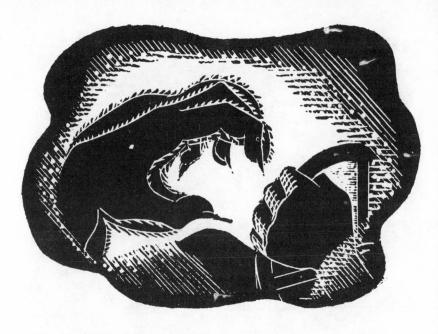

The Hairy Hands (*above*), from a woodcut by Theo Brown; (*below*)
the stretch of road they haunt

two small sisters lived in a "tied" farm cottage about a mile down the lane at the back of our house.

The youngest sister, then aged about six, suffered from inflamed and discharging eyes which had resisted all medical treatment. As a result, the child was unable to attend school and was out in the cottage garden one afternoon, when Mary Ann wandered by, looked over the gate and beckoned her. Reluctantly the child approached. Mary Ann, seizing her by the arm to prevent escape, exclaimed: "Oh, what sore eyes you've got, me dear" She then spat three times on each eye and went on her way. As might have been expected, the child immediately set up a yell for "Mam", who came hurrying out to investigate. When she realized the situation, she forbade the child to touch or wipe her eyes, thus evincing a respect for Mary Ann's abilities.

Very shortly, the child's eyes began to show a marked improvement. Inflammation subsided; eyelashes, which had been entirely absent until then, grew, and in a week or so she was attending school regularly with no more trouble.

The explanation? Hardly faith on the child's part, although she might possibly have been impressed by her mother's undoubted faith. Was it, once again, Mary Ann's ability to concentrate her will-force, or an exhibition of this mysterious natural gift of healing? Had the possible curative properties of saliva anything to do with it? Or was it all mere coincidence combined with the healing hand of time? Questions to which there are no answers, and this is but one example of many similar instances, some of which will be given in later chapters.

In 1970 a young business couple from London asked my help in finding a white witch to remove a curse. Unaccountable disasters had descended upon them after disagreement with a half-caste African employee whom they genuinely held to be responsible. Their detailed recital of events seemed incredibly remote from this age. Unfortunately witches claiming the ability to lift curses are now virtually non-existent.

CHAPTER EIGHTEEN

Magic Circles

THE circle has become a symbol of special significance in a diversity of cults, from ancient times down to the present. It represented the solar disc to the old sun-worshippers, and the full moon to the devotees of the lunar goddess. To Christians, the circle is emblematic of eternity, and it is also extensively used in witchcraft ritual, both ancient and modern.

The prehistoric ancestors of the witches and their religion, imbued with these beliefs, erected the great stone circles, still standing on Dartmoor today, as they have for the past 3,000 years. Even the contemporary little huts, built for everyday habitation were designed on the same pattern as perfect rings. Hundreds of their foundations are scattered over the hill-slopes, but never does one appear to have been misshapen, lop-sided, oval, oblong, square or rectangular, until at a later date the latter two forms occur of intent. Dwellings and so-called "sacred" circles alike are perfect rounds, as though drawn out on the turf with a giant compass.

Latter day witches, continuing the age-long cult, frequently made use of these old circles as meeting places, holding esbats, sabbats, and performing their ritual "ring" dances within the circumference of the tall granite stones (see Chapter 9).

Witchcraft and magic, although often confused in the public mind, are entirely separate cults having no connection and little real resemblance. The circle, however, figures prominently in each, the term "magic circle" being usually, although erroneously, used to describe a very old device traditionally used by black witches for bringing harm upon some enemy or disliked neighbour. No "magic" in the true sense of the word was ever employed by witches, but circles certainly were. Many odd tales of their efficacy are still related. Tales that belong mainly to a generation ago, but that are remembered and repeated by those of the present.

These "magic" circles, may be real or imaginary, that is to say, scratched with a knife or stick on turf or rock; chalked upon floor and doorstep, or the outline merely indicated by a pointing finger creating an invisible boundary. Another method, making use of the same device, was to rake the dead ashes on the hearth into a circle, within which the "curse" was solemnly laid.

As already mentioned, *modern* witch members of the recognized present-day societies are trained to concentrate will-force within the confines of a circle building up what they term a "cone of power". Nor can this store escape, for there is neither exit from the circle, nor entrance for alien penetration. Power, for good or for ill, according to its employment, lies within that thin encompassing line, but initiates alone know how to draw upon it.

In much the same way, during the last two or three years, the Aetherius Society has visited Dartmoor, among other places, for the purpose of "raising energy"—that is power—directed towards the prohibition of atom bomb tests and other causes. They consider certain hills, including Fur Tor to be natural reservoirs of this energy. *The Western Morning News* of 16 March, 1964, shows a photograph of members engaged in this energy-raising process on Holdstone Down near Combe Martin, a particularly favoured rendezvous. They stand *in a circle* with upraised hands palms upturned to the sky to enable them to draw and transmit this hidden energy from the centre of the earth through all their limbs, into the atmosphere. Their bodies, in fact, act as power-conductors. Circles, then, as what might be called safety devices for the storage of force, are of great importance, appearing in the ritual of many cults, ancient and modern. The normal village witch of yesterday, however, received no training, nor was even aware of the existence of organized centres of the craft. Nevertheless, according to stories told, and sometimes still believed, such witches were *naturally* adept in making use of magic circles to work off spite, often with alleged disastrous results to the victims.

Some typical instances of this peculiar art have been related to me from time to time, one by our late village postmistress who died just after the last war.

About a mile away, she remembered a reputed witch living on the edge of a Dartmoor common. For some reason she harboured a grudge against the girl who brought her milk daily from a neighbouring farm. So the woman traced the traditional circle in the middle of the only path leading to her cottage, by which the girl was bound to come, usually as her first morning caller. Unexpectedly, however, the witch's daughter, who was away in service in Okehampton, happened to arrive home early that morning and unsuspectingly stepped into the circle designed for the milk-girl. Shortly afterwards she became ill and died.

By contrast, the milk-girl who followed her a little later, remained unscathed.

From this and similar incidents it would appear that once the potent force is confined within the circle, its depositor exercises no further control over it. And, like the adder's bite, once the venom has been expended the emptied receptacle is rendered harmless.

When expedient, apparently a line—real or imaginary—could serve much the same purpose as a circle. I was told the following story by a woman whose grandmother, whom we will call Granny B, had figured in it as a child—which takes us back about four generations when credulity was stronger than it is today.

Then aged about seven, Granny B had been taken by *her* grandmother, Granny A, to glean in a cornfield. Among the gleaners was a reputed witch, who came up and begged for their gleanings. Being refused she became angry and swore that they should not leave the field until her request had been complied with. She then walked to the open gateway and with her finger deliberately traced an imaginary line across it. When Granny A. and grandchild went to leave the field, they found themselves halted at the wide open gateway, neither of them being able to proceed another step. Granny A. realizing the situation (probably she had watched the witch's performance) handed the child a pin, ordering her to creep up unseen behind the witch and stick it hard into her leg. Scared to death the child obeyed, then took to her heels and scuttled right out of the gate like a frightened rabbit followed, without the slightest difficulty by Granny A.

This drastic antidote, in shape of a pin, was in accordance with witch-lore, for, to draw a witch's blood, even a drop by a pin-prick, was said to break her spell rendering her harmless for the time being.

Of course, in this case, both grandmother and child had seen the imaginary barrier being raised, and were probably affected by something akin to mesmeric or hypnotic influence. Nevertheless, the spell worked, so did the antidote, while the anecdote is still handed down traditionally in the family's mental archives. Whatever the original facts, one thing is certain, that the child must have taken good care to keep clear of the old woman for a very long time afterwards.

In all ancient pagan religions, blood was recognized as the vital life-giving force. To drain away even the smallest drop had the same effect as draining away potency by breaking a magic-circle. In ritual sacrifices, the shedding of blood, human or animal, was solely for the purpose of revitalization and resurrection. Shed upon crops, it ensured their growth. Offered to a sun-god whose powers seemed to be declining at the winter solstice, it had the effect of "a shot in the arm", ensuring his re-appearance later in undiminished strength. Poured out upon the sea, blood guaranteed a good fish harvest, survivals of these ceremonies being still observed in various religious services for "blessing the boats" or in the quaint events, including skipping, which are enacted every February upon the beach at Scarborough.

In the Kingsteignton ram-roasting feast, annually celebrated in May, the ram's blood was originally an offering to a river-god who seemed to be withholding water supplies. The more blood that flowed, the more water would also flow—an idea that crops up again in the blood-stopping charms. With blood transfusions being widely carried out today, who shall say that the old beliefs in the potency of blood were so wide of the mark?

Another story of circle magic comes from the Warren House Inn, centre of an area rich in archaeological, legendary and folklore interest.

Two men, Will and Tom, quarrelled over their drinks one night, and Tom threatened that he would complete the other's life-circle. A few evenings later as Will stood in the crowded bar with his back to the door, Tom approaching unseen, managed to draw a chalk-line on the floor, round his unwitting victim's feet. The result, of course followed the usual pattern—sudden illness and death. This, I was told, was not due to shock or mental strain, but to the violent onslaught of a hitherto unsuspected malignant disease. Perhaps, therefore, coincidence played some part in this case.

There are other stories similar to that of the milk-girl and the witch's unfortunate daughter. In the village where the rector believed black magic still to be practised, I heard the following:

A woman there having "had words" with a workman, surreptitiously prepared a magic circle on one side of a stile which he regularly crossed on his way to work. Unknown to the witch, somebody caught sight of her preparations, guessed their purpose, and warned the intended victim. Next morning the man set out along the field path as usual, but took with him a live hen. Before climbing the stile, he threw the bird over to the other side where the witch had been seen at work. "Immediately," said my story-teller, "that hen turned over on its back with its two legs sticking up in the air, stone-dead."

Sometimes a dog has trotted ahead of its owner in similar circumstances, receiving the circle's curse, and has thus saved his master's life.

The interest here lies not in the number of such tales, but in the fact that they are still remembered, related, and to all appearances, accepted. They are usually given as occurrences of the near past, not of the present, for then there would be no hint or reference to them.

A magic circle was used for a rather different purpose not long ago on the top of Kestor Rock, the incident being related to me by Ernest, a Chagford moorman of complete hard-headedness and reliability.

He was accompanying another local resident, George, on a search for some missing sheep one bright spring afternoon when, to obtain a wider view of the surrounding moor, they climbed to the top of Kestor. There, curled up asleep on the sun-warmed granite lay a viper. George approached and slowly and deliberately with his walking-stick, traced an imaginary ring round the creature, at the same time muttering some words which Ernest "couldn't rightly hear". Nor would George repeat them upon request later. The circle completed, George poked up the adder. It darted towards the two men, but stopped dead when it reached the imaginary line. Then—and here Ernest assured me that "he'd nivver have believed sich a thing, if he hadn't see'd it with his own eyes"—that snake crawled round and round inside its boundary line, desperately seeking an exit from the circle that wasn't there. I asked how long this continued, before it finally broke through, but Ernest replied laconically: "Us didn't wait to see, us just went on."

Here we have another tale with no rational explanation unless it can be found in the word "suggestion". Possibly the apparently sleeping viper was, in reality, watching out of the corner of its eye George's stick going round and round, giving it the hypnotic feeling that it was being enclosed. Whether one can credit a snake with that amount of imagination is another question. Possibly again, this Dartmoor man possessed faculties akin to those of an Eastern snake-charmer, these mysterious gifts being universal. Analagous to this incident is an old belief that a live hen may be safely tethered to the ground simply by being carried round a magic circle with its beak to the circumference. I have no first-hand knowledge of this particular device but feel that if snakes can be thus deluded. so presumably might hens.

CHAPTER NINETEEN

The Evil Eye

ILL-WISHING and the use of magic circles are recognized tools of the black witch's trade, as was the practice of sticking pins or thorns into a sheep's heart to cause, by a process of sympathetic magic, equivalent pain or disease to the human heart it was supposed to represent. Of this process, and of the modelling of clay figurines for a like purpose, I have had no personal experience, and believe that this particular bit of black witchcraft has long since died out.

As we have already seen, however, in certain parts of Devon belief in the efficacy of ill-wishing still lingers although to a diminishing extent, being more prevalent in the western than in the eastern districts of the county. Magic circles are still occasionally used—if only to encompass snakes and hens—but belief in the ability to over-look with the "evil eye", as distinct from ill-wishing or cursing, is, as far as I know, also a thing of the past. Only once have I come across an *authentic* case—if that is the right word—and the particular occurrence was at least thirty odd years ago.

At that time, an uncle of ours was rector of a remote Devonshire country parish, comprising a village and two hamlets, each with its separate church. These were served faithfully by their pastor who rode between them on horseback or drove in a pony-trap until the last years of his life when a car was substituted. He was a well-read man of culture, an Oxford scholar, a naturalist and writer. He was also about the last of the old-fashioned "squarsons", being lord of the manor, owning the advowson of his living, farming his glebe, and taking part in all country sports for over forty years, during the latter part of which time he seldom left his parish, even for a day. It might, perhaps, therefore be questioned to what extent he absorbed some of the ideas of the circumscribed community of which he was an integral part.

Indeed, he might be said to have become its hub and focus, for he was a true "father" to his flock who brought all their problems of everyday life to him for solution. Apart from parochial duties, he was consulted on legal matters, drew up wills and settled disputes, often also acting in the capacity of medical adviser. As if these varied rôles were not enough for any one man he was also a white witch, possessor of the natural healing gift which he used for charming warts, adder-bite and ring-worm.

Having a white witch in the family should have presented us with a golden opportunity of obtaining an insight into the workings of this elusive power. But like all such practitioners, he refused to discuss the subject. In his own words, he felt that should he do so "the virtue would leave him", recalling Christ's words in the New Testament, to a woman who surreptitiously touched the hem of his garment. It was Uncle Rector who related the following incident of over-looking, having witnessed it himself.

Stables, coach-house, shippens and pigsties, all with their full complement of inhabitants had to be passed by anyone visiting the rectory by the back drive. One day a young woman came to lay some problem before this man of many parts, accompanied by her mother, a woman at whom many of her neighbours looked askance. As the rector walked down the drive with them after the interview, the mother suddenly stopped beside a sty containing a sow and her litter. Pointing her finger at one little pig she exclaimed: "Oh, the pretty little pig! Oh, the pretty little dear!" Whereupon, according to Uncle Rector's eye-witness account, the piglet selected for this attention rolled over upon its back, dead. The daughter, apparently accustomed to this disconcerting behaviour on the part of her parent, pulled her away and scolded her saying: "Now, Mother, come away.

You didn't ought ter 'a done that to parson's pig." Nor could we elicit any further comments from Uncle Rector as to what construction he himself placed upon the incident thus related.

This remarkable man died in 1939 and is buried in the familiar surroundings of his own little churchyard beside his wife, two sons, a daughter, and a daughter-in-law.

Many years ago, my husband was well acquainted with a farmer and his son both of whom were perpetually at loggerheads with a poacher, Tom, reputed to be a black witch. His threats of reprisals were regarded by both father and son with a genuine, primitive fear.

Walking up a long hill one day my husband came upon the farmer and his wife standing in the middle of the road beside their trap, between the shafts of which their old cob lay prostrate.

While doing what he could to help, my husband was subjected to a tirade against poacher Tom, who, the farmer swore, had over-looked his horse. Apart from any over-looking by Tom, what the couple themselves had overlooked was the fact that the poor old nag was long past work and due for collapse at any time. But in the farmer's mind, the *certainty* of this over-looking was too genuine to admit any doubt.

Not long after this mishap, the farmer's son Jim happened upon one of the poacher's gins. He promptly confiscated both it and the rabbit it contained, just as Tom came creeping up under the hedge to collect his spoils. Vituperation ensued, dire threats of reprisals being hurled after Jim as he went off to his ploughing. Later that afternoon he, like the trap-horse, collapsed, and was found lying on the furrows having had some unaccountable fit or seizure.

Now, both Jim and his father were *genuinely* scared of the poacher, being convinced of his "black" abilities. Possibly, therefore, in Jim's case, his sudden seizure might have been caused by sheer fright. This, of course, would not apply to the old cob, although here the verdict might well have been "collapse from natural causes".

These incidents occurred, of course, well in the past, but their interest lies in the fact that they all took place well within not-so-old living memory.

It used to be thought that the *first* direct glance from the eye of a black witch intending harm contained the baleful influence. If this could be diverted so also would disaster. As we have seen, most witchcraft tricks could be met by recognized anti-dotes. To prevent the possibility of over-looking, it was only necessary to direct the glance elsewhere. This intention lay behind the coloured glass "witch-balls" hung in cottage windows; the garlands of flowers or bright berried branches nailed above the stable and cowshed doors or placed round the necks of cattle. Even a bright buttonhole was sometimes worn to serve the same purpose. All were in the nature of red herrings to attract this important first glance. Certain plants were considered especially efficacious as witch-preventatives and if the selection contained dill, vervain, mountain-ash (quick beam in the West Country), elder, St. John's wort, or trefoil (the latter being emblematic of the Trinity), the result was likely to be proportionately more satisfactory.

This ancient belief has an exceedingly interesting modern corollary, which suggests that many a ridiculed superstition and old wives' tale may, indeed, contain a possible half-brick of fact in its foundations.

In his book *Witchcraft Today*, G. B. Gardner tells us that in March 1956 a radiothesia journal, *The Pendulum*, published an account of a lecture given by professor Otto Raher of Cornell University, U.S.A., to a gathering of scientists. During its course, he described how yeast cells could be killed *by the glance of a person looking at them intently for a few minutes*. The explanation given was that certain rays emitted from the human eye as well as from other parts of the body *can cause actual physical change*.

If capable of proof and development, this experiment links up in a remarkable way with some of the oldest witchcraft tenets, long dismissed as superstitious nonsense. The whole puzzling subject of witchcraft and its mysterious beliefs, gifts and powers, was, I think, aptly commented upon in a paragraph which appeared in *The Western Morning News* of 18 April, 1961.

It seems unlikely that the idea . . . would have survived so long unless there had been something in it. The fact that natural forces can be used before people find scientifically what they are is not a case for dismissing them as imaginary. If it were, we should know nothing now about electricity and the structure of matter. Until the medical profession can prove that faith-healers do harm to patients, it should be cautious of interfering, beyond requiring that visits should be at the patient's request.

Although the above lines referred mainly to the subject of faith-healing, they apply equally to the whole wide range of these inexplicable powers, undoubtedly possessed by certain individuals. If these powers may be used beneficially it seems only logical to assume that they are capable also of being employed malevolently. From the fact, however, that black witchcraft and belief in it is certainly becoming a thing of the past, one may infer that this is not necessarily from any impossibility of practice, but because the desire to work—or to pretend to work—secret harm is incompatible with the more enlightened outlook of the present day. Whatever the nature of the power, it is being increasingly directed towards good. Examples of the remarkable results obtained by local charmers, white witches, healers—call them what you will—are given in the next two chapters.*

* See Postscript *Modern Village Charmers* p. 191.

CHAPTER TWENTY

Warts and Ring-worm

I T is perhaps strange, that the "evil eye", powerful weapon of black witchcraft, seems to have no counterpart in white witchery, there being no record, as far as I know, of a white witch over-looking with a benevolent eye. Possibly this process takes place in cases where white witches, having merely glanced at warts or ring-worms announce simply: "They'll go." And they do. If this is so, the fact is never stated, and there is no recognized beneficial counterpart to the "evil eye". The term "blessing" however, used synonymously for "charming", may originally have been applied in its literal sense namely, to bestow a blessing as opposed to a curse. For although doubt may exist as to the abilities of black witches, there can be none whatever about the benefits derived from the white art.

Visitors to the West Country are astonished and often frankly incredulous when they hear accounts of "charming" in this day and age. Those of us who have lived beside it for many years hold a different opinion, having had too many proofs of its success to be left doubting. Almost every village and many a town still has its natural healer, a man or woman whom people consult as openly as they would their doctor or vet, humans and animals alike being brought to have their ailments charmed away. Sometimes, even a personal visit is unnecessary, intimation of the need by telephone being all that is required for remedial measures to be put into immediate operation. Local doctors, indeed, more often than not unsuccessful in the removal of warts, frequently send their patients to Mr. A. or Mr. B. who charms for warts in a neighbouring village.

We had rather an amusing demonstration of this last spring, when a woman walked into our village stores asking to be directed to the "witch-doctor who lives in Sticklepath". She was sent along to us—not because we can lay claim to inclusion in the ranks of this interesting fraternity—but because it was thought that we might be able to help.

At first our visitor appeared slightly hesitant and embarrassed, being obviously unused to the procedure, but eventually explained her quest. She was seeking the "witch-doctor" at the instigation of one of Okehampton's medical practitioners by whom she had been unsuccessfully treated for a painful wart on the sole of her foot. He had advised her in the end to visit this man, who had, so he told her, cured his own children "by laying his hoary finger on their warts". Owing to some slight misunderstanding, she had confused the villages and come to the wrong one. At present there is no white witch in Sticklepath. We were, however, able to direct her to the man she was seeking, in the next Dartmoor village. Open inquiry for a "witch-doctor" at the present date certainly might strike some people as incongruous.

By a curious coincidence, only recently, as I was writing this account of witchcraft-healing, I happened to talk to a man whose young daughter had been suffering apparently from the same complaint, an outbreak of verrucas, or in-growing warts, on the soles of her feet. *And*, the same doctor had suggested that she went to the same healer, who, through a long period of years has successfully charmed many people, as well as horses, cattle and dogs.

"You know him of course?" the father asked me. I replied that I did and then heard the result of the consultation.

Father and daughter had gone together by appointment, but the girl had been taken into another room alone. The charmer touched the soles of her feet (with the same hoary finger?) said "some words", and the cure was complete. "There isn't even one scar left to show where they've been," ended her father's account.

These are typical of quite common occurrences in this part of Devon, where I heard of a somewhat similar instance from a young farmer's wife, lately settled in the county. The couple, fresh from agricultural college training, have taken a farm near a small village. Hardly were they established when a ring-worm outbreak affected their dairy herd. They immediately telephoned the official Ministry of Agriculture vet whose response left them both amazed and perplexed. "If you're living at R," he said, "you don't need me. You've got Mr. C practically next door. He'll charm your cows for you."

Living in Rome, the couple conformed to Roman standards —not without some understandable initial hesitation—and the ring-worm disappeared.

For some as yet inexplicable reason which is completely baffling, all white witches are adepts in wart-curing. To a white witch indeed this alleviation seems to be almost child's play, the first and most elementary stage of the art. This is the more curious as doctors are notoriously unsuccessful in this particular field, sometimes, as already mentioned, sending their patients on to some local white witch.

Another curious fact about wart-charming is the variety of methods employed by these healers. There is no one standard cure, nor are herbal remedies often used. Each practitioner, apparently, acts in accordance with individual idea or whim. To list the numerous and varied ways by which these cures are effected would require far too much space, but a few may be described here. One of the most common is achieved by the mere shaking of hands as practised by the well-known Exeter market white witch mentioned in Chapter 16. Another is for the healer to *buy* the patient's warts for ½d. In some cases the coin must be carefully preserved or the warts will return. In others, the opposite is enjoined, and the coin must be thrown away at once, the warts being abandoned with the coin.

A farmer-neighbour, one of the most hard-headed practical and sceptical men I have ever known, suffered from warts covering both hands. Out hunting one day, he happened to meet a noted wart-charmer who commented upon the disfigurement, remarking casually: "I'll give 'ee halfpenny for 'em, boy!" The farmer merely laughed, but said he would accept the ½d., although he considered the man a "proper old fraud". The coin changed pockets, after which the farmer dismissed the incident altogether from his mind, until one day, to his surprise he found both hands clear of the warts from which he had suffered for so many years. He was sufficiently impressed to take his young daughter, similarly afflicted, to the same man, the result being equally successful. No question of faith entered this transaction—unless it was on the part of the white witch. Until the accomplished cure of both himself and his daughter, the farmer remained sceptical throughout. After that, certainly, he became a reluctant convert.

Some witches advocate rubbing warts (usually pronounced *wurts* in the vernacular) with bean-pods, others with bacon-rind. In each case pods and rinds must be buried immediately after application. As they decay, so will the warts, the reasoning here presumably being based upon sympathetic magic. Results, however, appear to be equally satisfactory proving that the actual *methods* employed can have little or no bearing on the subsequent cure.

Not long ago, a friend told me that an old cottage on their property had just been demolished, after the death of a tenant reputed to be a witch. When the floorboards were ripped up piles of rat-gnawed bacon-rinds were unearthed, obviously the residue of the old lady's charms. At the time, however, local opinion considered them to be sinister proofs of the witch's black magic.

Bean pods figure in another curious incident related by a country parson. A reputed witch had died in his parish, and during the time in which her body lay in the kitchen-living-room of her cottage there occurred curious manifestations,

L

which he himself witnessed. Showers of bean-pods kept falling down the chimney on to the empty hearth. Investigation of both chimney and roof were made, but everything appeared normal. Yet the pods continued to fall at intervals until the funeral, after which they ceased as mysteriously as they had started.

The broad bean plant makes a frequent appearance in witch-lore, although not one white witch, assiduously applying its pods to warts today, is aware of why she does so. Witchcraft, it will be remembered, is a moon-cult; all white, and especially sweet-scented flowers were dedicated to the White Goddess. Lilies-of-the-valley, hawthorn, white lilac and beans showed palely, and shed their perfume in the May dusk as covens gathered for a sabbat. Even the white "swad" lining a bean-pod, counted as an extra attribute, a double dedication as it were. Whether in addition this lining possesses any remedial properties is doubtful, remembering that the same results are achieved with bacon-rinds, beef, a green elder stick, and other agents in a similar way. No, the bean is firmly rooted in a remote past, and its continuing link with witchcraft practice is a very interesting survival.

At a meeting recently, I sat next to a young woman who told me that her father charms warts by rubbing them with beef, after which, of course, like rinds and pods, the meat must be buried.

"Mr. L opposite us wanted Dad to do his warts this week-end," confided the girl, "but Mrs. L had got a bit of pork for Sunday's dinner, so t'was no good. Dad says it must be beef, so she's going to get some this week-end and Dad'll do them then instead."

It seems that in these days of expensive joints, the patient is expected to provide his own "cut".

Occasionally some practitioner with a sense of the dramatic or the artistic is encountered. A Dartmoor woman described how, when a child, she was taken to have her warts cured "by an old lady who lived at Holne". She was required to pay three visits, taking with her a black-thorn, wool from a white sheep, and milk from a red cow. The white witch kept the thorn and the wool but the milk was proffered fresh every time. (Possibly a useful addition to the larder.) The witch-woman held the thorn, dipped the wool in the milk and anointed the warts— with the expected sequel that they disappeared. Possibly this artistically or theatrically-minded witch was out to impress as well as to cure.

Counting plays a part in several of the methods used. By some witches the patient is instructed to go home, count his warts and put the equivalent number of small stones or pebbles into a bag which he must then throw away, preferably at a cross-roads. I know a woman now about fifty, who, when in her twenties, adopted this procedure. At the time, she explained to me the danger of picking up any package found lying by the wayside. If, however, curiosity overcame caution, the packet should be kicked first to ascertain its contents, for should it contain "wart stones", the finder would automatically transfer to himself someone else's discarded warts.

One of the best wart-counting stories I have heard was told me by the daughter of an old-time squire. Both his hands had been peppered with persistent warts for years, every possible remedy having been tried unavailingly. Walking home from church one Sunday, he overtook an old village neighbour with whom he joined company. Presently, with characteristic directness, the old man commented on the squire's disfigurement. "How many wurts have 'ee got then, zur?" he asked. The squire counted, "Twenty-seven." "They'll go," was the response, and no more was said on the subject. At home relating this incident to his wife, she exclaimed, "You haven't as many warts as *that*, surely!" He counted again. "Actually I've got one more," he said, "I told old Charlie twenty-seven, but it's twenty-eight."

Very shortly, twenty-seven warts had disappeared without trace. One remained.

After this story, one can understand that the white witch

who insists on beef for his charming, also insists on counting his patient's warts himself.

Similar in essentials is a case of ring-worm charming. A young farm-hand described how a year or so ago, he had several ring-worms on his hand, caught from the cattle in his care. He went to his own village white witch, who looked at his hands and asked how many patches he had. The lad gave the number and was told he would have no more trouble with them. Nor did he, but upon undressing that night he discovered several new rings of which he had been unaware, on his back. In a few days time, those on his hands had gone while those on his back persisted.

These "counting cures" are among the most mystifying. If the basis of the healing-gift is intense will-concentration, judging by these stories, it would seem as though concentration must be brought to bear on each separate wart or ring-worm. Surely an impossibility; or, if feasible, enough to drain the "virtue" out of the hardiest healer. One wart-charmer refuses to treat more than one person at a time, because, in his own words, "It takes too much out of me." How much more would it take out of a man to concentrate on a number of warts, one by one!

By contrast, a year ago I talked to an ex-district nurse, who, in her retirement, now charms for the usual minor ailments. The charm was given to her, not inherited, but she found herself able to use it successfully. Its accompanying words are a direct prayer in Biblical phraseology, the exact nature of which she did not reveal. Probably it resembled most of the stereotyped doggerels which are given in Chapter 22. Complete faith on her part is essential, but not necessarily on the part of the patient. Nor, she assured me, has the exercise of this gift any adverse effect upon her—in contrast to the usual experiences of other healers.

In this instance, what might be termed *semi*-faith appears to be enough, that is belief on one side, but not upon the other. If this provides a workable basis, it would account for the response of children and animals to treatment. One is, however, no nearer a real solution of the secret behind these mysterious powers. Perhaps Shaw Desmond's definition is as near as any at present, confirming to some extent the claims of the witches themselves. In *Psychic Pitfalls* he writes: Witchcraft is simply thought transference or telepathy. If no *thought* could be passed from one person to another, there could be no healing.

CHAPTER TWENTY-ONE

Other Cures

CONSIDERING that natural healers or white witches achieve an almost 100 per cent success with their charming, it is strange that so much apparently serious concentration and will-force should be directed solely to the healing of relatively minor ailments. So astonishingly successful are these cures that one would expect their range to be extended to disorders of a graver character—migraine, dyspepsia, rheumatism or even malignant growths. If some types of ailment respond readily to charming, why not others? At present the range appears to be limited and almost standardized—warts, ring-worm, bleeding, burns, thorns, chilblains, toothache, ear-ache and snake-bite comprising most of the repertoire.

Were the witches' abilities directed solely to mental or psychological relief it would be more comprehensible. But on the contrary, with the same faith that can remove mountains, they remove bodily excrescences such as warts, carbuncles and "cauliflower ears". Why not, therefore, an internal growth? If pain can be charmed from an aching tooth, why not the rheumatic pains from an aching limb? No serious attempts of this kind seem to be tried, unless perhaps by accredited faith-healers in an altogether different walk of life.

Perhaps the natural untrained healer is capable only of obtaining surface or near surface reactions as opposed to those that are more deeply-rooted. That, I believe, is the opinion of many doctors.

Each complaint in which a white witch specializes has its accompanying word-charm. These of course vary slightly, having been handed down traditionally, like all folklore, from one generation to the next. Rather unusually, I have heard of a woman who cures erysipelas, and of a man who charms for shingles—both of which might be called "surface ailments", like ring-worm.

The shingle-healer's method was described to me by a woman whose husband had just been cured of a painful attack in his head, face and neck.

This white witch lives in North Devon where he prefers to receive the sufferer. Should a patient be too ill to travel, however, he will visit him at home where the same procedure takes place.

The charmer twines together a wreath or ring of rushes which he places over the affected area of skin, after which the ring is hung up *inside* his chimney. Three visits must be paid, the same process being repeated on each occasion. There was no mention of any accompanying words, nor do I know of a "shingle charm".

Two points may be commented upon here. First, a question as to whether the time lag between the three visits would be of sufficient length to allow of natural recovery. Secondly, in the wreath of rushes we undoubtedly see the magic-circle again, the affected spot upon which the healer concentrates being confined within that boundary ring.

Since writing the above paragraph, I have been told by a friend of another case of shingle-charming, the practitioner in this case being a woman living in Torrington.

On Easter Day, 1964, my friend was rung up by their district nurse who was suffering from a similar acute attack of shingles in her head and face. None of the remedies prescribed by doctors bringing any alleviation, the pain was such, that although it was Easter Sunday morning, she begged to be driven into Torrington to the "charmer". The latter, advised of their coming, took the nurse indoors, and carrying a bunch of *rushes* walked round her in a *circle*. Three visits were, again, to be paid, but after the first, at about 7 o'clock on Easter Day evening, the patient's agonizing pain suddenly ceased. She herself described the feeling as of having an oppressive lid suddenly removed from the top of her head. Nevertheless, she paid the remaining two prescribed visits. On the last occasion she was kept waiting a short time, the charmer explaining the delay as having been caused because she had been obliged to go out to cut more rushes.

It will be noted that rushes—of no particular specified sort— probably out of the nearest marsh seem to be essential in each case. Another similar feature is the circle. A circle of rushes was used by the man witch; a circle was paced round her patient by the woman. The magic circle in operation once more.

After warts and ring-worm, blood-stopping, or "blessing for bleeding", is perhaps most commonly practised particularly upon cattle who have been fighting and "horned" each other.

Some years ago we lived in a small village composed mainly of a simple agricultural community. Two young bachelor farmers, close friends and now retired elderly men, often sent to a third farmer and neighbour, a well-known charmer, when accidents of this sort occurred among their beasts. They sent *to* and not *for* the man, nothing else being necessary. The white witch never visited the injured animal. On receiving a message for help (delivered by bicycle in those days) he retired alone into a room, "said some words" and as far as anyone knew, that was all that took place.

One of these young bachelors had the blood-stopping charm in his family where it had been handed down according to tradition, from male to female alternately in each generation. His mother was at that time the official holder, but neither she nor any of her sons were endowed with the gift of using it. It was, therefore, copied out for me—the copy is still in my possession—and is given, among others, in the next chapter.

Incidentally, I knew two white witches a few years ago who gave their services in the same way as the blood-charming farmer, but by telephone. One charmed for bleeding, the other for warts and ring-worm. You rang up, stated your need, and no more was required.

Belief in the ability of a white witch to arrest a flow of blood —sometimes with malignant intent—was deep-rooted. A few years ago a neighbouring farmer was having a pig killed in his yard. To ensure good white meat, it was customary for pigs to be well bled. On this occasion, at the critical moment, a well-known blood-charmer happened to pass by, pausing, as any countryman would, to watch the proceedings. Seeing him looking over the wall, the farmer peremptorily ordered him off. "Just for safety," he said afterwards, "I wasn't going to risk him spoiling my pig-meat." In other words, he feared that the man's blood-stopping ability might be exercised at the wrong moment.

By the reasoning of sympathetic magic one essential for success in blood-stopping is that no running water must lie between white-witch and patient, otherwise, as the witch crossed flowing water, so would the staunched blood start flowing again. Should a white witch be on his way home, having charmed a patient, he must at all costs avoid crossing a stream, even if that necessitates a detour of several miles. Should he fail to do so, the success of the cure would be negatived.

Rather an odd story comes again from the village mentioned before, where the rector believed black magic to be practised. Here I was told of a farmer who employed an unskilled man to perform a slight surgical operation on a cow's leg. During the process the knife slipped, and the wound thus made continued to bleed profusely. The angry farmer ordered the man to go immediately for a woman who lived nearby, and who "blessed for bleeding". She arrived, said her charm, but the wound continued to bleed. Completely puzzled she said to the farmer: "If you cut this cow's leg, it should have stopped bleeding by now." The farmer explained that he had not been responsible.

"Well!" exclaimed the witch, somewhat annoyed. "Why didn't 'ee tell me that before? I charmed thinking 'twas *you* who done it. Now I'll have to do it all over again." Which she did, with consequent cessation of the flow of blood.

This incident reveals an interesting and unusual aspect of charming. According to this it would seem that a witch's power must be directed—in some cases, at least—not only to the injured patient, but also to the person responsible for that injury.

We have another example of sympathetic magic in an old Dartmoor remedy for chilblains. To get rid of them, according to a friend's domestic help, it is only necessary to *wish them on to a person just dead*. The woman assured our friend that during last winter's extreme cold, she had removed her own by this simple method. Here the sympathetic link is between the coldness of the chilblain, and the coldness of the dead body— like being attracted to like. The belief that by seriously *wishing* an ailment upon another person it will be thus transferred is current today.

Meeting an acquaintance in the village shop during a cold spell, I inquired after her daughter's sore throat, adding that I hoped she hadn't given it to her mother, meaning, of course, passed on the germ. "No," replied my acquaintance confidently, "she hasn't done it yet because she's still got it." The inference being that until the girl *chose* to part with it, her mother would remain immune.

My husband, suffering from a bad cold, was once walking on Dartmoor with an elderly moorman and voiced the hope that he would not pass the cold on to his companion. Old John was genuinely shocked—and rather hurt. "Oh, no, sir, please don't do that," he begged. "I don't want it. You wouldn't do a thing like that, would 'ee now?" To him, obviously, the transference of a cold had nothing to do with a possible stray germ, but constituted a deliberate act, equivalent to a deed of gift which the recipient was powerless to refuse. The implied inference is on a par with the discarding of wart-pebbles in order that they may be transferred to the unsuspecting finder. Underlying this idea, too, is the fundamental witch-belief in the power of will and thought transference.

Judging from these two incidents, even the ordinary individual, laying no claim to witchcraft practices, is considered capable of passing on an unwanted complaint to another person, merely by evincing a strong enough desire to do so. This gives rise to interesting reflections as to the latent power in any one of us, but beyond an obvious necessity for will-exertion, no question of charming is involved.

Returning to authentic charming, I was sitting on the platform of a village hall one afternoon with several other women. After the meeting the official next to me pulled up her sleeve displaying a great red scald mark extending from elbow to wrist. "I only did it the day before yesterday," she informed me, "and I haven't put a thing on it. I can bless for burns, you know, and as soon as I'd upset the boiling pan over my arm, I just sat down, passed my other hand up and down over the scald, said the charm, and it's been all right since."

She had no inhibition about repeating the words of the charm which I wrote down there and then, and give, among those in the next chapter. This was certainly a case of "physician, heal thyself", brought to a satisfactory conclusion.

Thorns are also charmed out of festering fingers or feet, but I have met only one woman who specializes in this particular branch. She was charming in 1961 and presumably still does so. Her reason for making the initial experiment was unusual. Her mother, she told me, had died from blood-poisoning caused by a blackthorn, after which tragedy she felt a compulsion to prevent the same fate befalling anyone else. From a white witch she obtained the charm which consists (as usual) of "some words from the Bible", but it will not work unless the patient has faith. In which case the woman's ministrations could be considered as true faith-healing which the majority of charmings are not, especially when children and animals are concerned—together, indeed, with a number of very sceptical adults. Faith of some sort, however, must always be present in the healer, or no cure could result.

In former years, faith and "words" were often supplemented by a sloughed viper skin, to aid thorn extraction—one more example of sympathetic magic. A snake's skin is "drawn" off at the appropriate season, as the reptile rubs its length along rushes or herbage. Therefore, it was reasoned, the discarded skin would also possess the power of "drawing" out thorns or splinters. This seems to be a fairly straightforward chain of thought, but oddly enough the skin was to be applied to that part of the hand opposite the embedded thorn, which would then be *repelled* into a natural withdrawal.

The following charm, given as an example of a really old and more than usually illiterate type, is one quoted in Vol. XXXI of the *Transactions of the Devonshire Association* copied verbatim from some old papers found at Marystowe towards the end of the last century:

Charm for a Thorn. When Christ was upon middle earth, he was prick, his blood sprung unto heaven, it shall neither runkle, canker or rust—neither shall they blood (then name the person's name) they do it for and say in the name of the father and of the Son and of the holy ghost.

The illiteracy of these charms is, in fact, an indication of their extreme age. Some definitely date back to the pre-Conquest era, having been found in Anglo-Saxon MSS. To the pagan population of early times they indubitably had great significance, but like so much else, when adopted and given a Christian veneer by the Church, meaning became lost or obscure. This accounts to a great degree, for the often meaningless and ungrammatical jumble of words through which one can just glimpse the underlying concept.

CHAPTER TWENTY-TWO

Charms

"A WITCH performs no rite, utters no spell, possesses no medicine. An act of witchcraft is a psychic act." writes Evans Pritchard in *Witchcraft, Oracles and Magic among the Azande*.

The same idea is expressed by Dr. M. Field, in his work *Religion and Medicine of the Gā People*, when he says: "Witchcraft among a Gold Coast tribe . . . has no palpable apparatus connected with it; no rites, ceremonies, incantations or invocations that the witch has to perform. It is simply projected at will from the mind of the witch. . . . Witches are people afflicted with the obsession that they have the power to harm others by *thinking* them harm."

Both authors were discussing witchcraft among primitive tribes, but witchcraft is a universal belief, the most ancient religion in the world. With slight variations, what holds good for witchcraft in Africa, Mexico or Borneo also holds good for what remains of it in Britain today. Certainly it might be applied to trained witches of the seven or so officially recognized witch societies still in existence, although some ritual and ceremony plays a part in their cult. Possibly, however, today these are of social rather than of "working" significance.

It may also be logically assumed, that if "obsession" with the power to harm obtains, so also must the reverse intention when good rather than evil is the objective, as in cases of healing.

As regards the ordinary *natural* village witch, he or she uses, as far as can be seen, little or no ritual. Occasionally an act of showmanship is staged, as with the black thorn, white wool, and red cow wart-cure, described in Chapter 20. On the other hand a little staging may be of assistance in obtaining a better result. It would create a greater impression of ability in the patient's mind, the waters of Abana and Pharpar being always more desirable than those of Israel.

It would, however, be untrue to say that no spell is uttered. What are the "muttered words" or "some words out of the Bible", but the recognized charms which almost invariably accompany a white witch's healing act? Today's charms and blessings are but yesterday's old-fashioned spells mumbled by the fairy-tale witch. It should be remembered that this prominent character was merely a distorted edition of her real-life medieval counterpart.

Invocations in the form of definite prayer, spells or charms have always been an integral part of the natural healer's art. Their content remained a closely guarded secret, known only to the practitioner until, in due course, it was handed on to the next generation. As mentioned in the last chapter, this, too, was directed by protocol. It passed from man to woman in alternate generations until some member of the correct sex was found to possess "the gift". Not so long ago this convention was strictly adhered to; latterly, as old customs lapse in more sophisticated districts, the secret words of some of these charms have leaked out or been disclosed by people who today consider them as nothing more than "a lot of old rubbish".

Quite frankly, upon reading them, one cannot but agree. Taking the *Charm for Thorn*, given at the end of the last chapter as an example, the words are obviously the products of primitive uneducated minds, a jumble of illiterate doggerel based on Biblical phraseology; ungrammatical, unpunctuated and mis-spelt. One feels that any old abracadabra would answer the purpose equally well, as probably it would. Their illiteracy has interest, as being a criterion of their age and of the fact that they have been more or less faithfully learned or copied and handed down through a very long period. Here and there, as educational standards improved, a copyist amended spelling or inserted punctuation, but no material alterations have been made, the gist of the matter remaining the same.

Below are a few typical examples of some of the charms in common use both yesterday and today, there being no indication as to their age or origin. The first is copied from the paper on which it was written down for me in 1929 by the mother of the young bachelor farmer who did not himself possess "the gift".

Blessing for Stopping Blood

Christ our Lord was born in Bethlehem. He was baptized in the river of Jordan. The waters wild and rude. He bid it to stand and it stood.
So shall the Blood of (Mrs. Gordon) be still
In the Name of the Father and the Son and Holy Ghost.

Amen.

Say this three times three.
Praise God may all things pass away.

This I believe, might be called a "regulation" charm, used, with slight verbal alteration by the many white witches who bless for bleeding. The same applies to the *Charm for Burns*, but here it is possible to give a comparison between an older and the present versions. William Crossing in *Folk Rhymes of Devon* quotes it thus:

> Three Angels came from North, East and West
> One brought fire, another brought frost
> And the third brought the Holy Ghost.
> So out fire and in frost.
> In the name of the Father, Son and Holy Ghost.

As repeated to me seven years ago by the woman who had recited it when healing her own scalded arm, the charm ran:

> Three Angels came out of the South
> One was fire, one was frost and one was the Holy Ghost,
> Out fire, in frost.
> In the name of the Father, Son and Holy Ghost.

Very little verbal difference, whilst the actual pattern or underlying sentiment remains precisely the same. One notes that in
the more "modern" version, only *one* point of the compass is
named, that being the *south* oddly enough, the one omitted in
the earlier form. Probably the substitution was accidental rather
than intentional, a lapse of memory in repetition.

Very rarely do these charmers fail with their varying methods
and their similar abracadabra. In fact I have heard of only two
failures to cure, out of scores of successes.

One occurred not long ago, when a woman had her warts
blessed by a very well-known and usually successful healer,
but this time to no avail. This is extremely unusual, but
may perhaps be attributed to the fact that the man is growing
old, and his general abilities declining. As so few failures occur,
it seems probable that when a white witch becomes conscious
of a weakening in power, he refuses further applications and
quietly withdraws into obscurity.

The second and very glaring case of failure happened at
Belstone many years ago now, when the site of the present
Brennamoor Hotel was the cottage dwelling of a white witch.
My informant was a child at the time but well remembered the
incident which caused a considerable stir.

A girl with a badly burned arm had, in the usual way, been
taken to the white witch, who went into her garden, dug up a
couple of earth worms and *sewed them into the raw flesh of
the burn*. At the same time she "muttered some words"—
probably a conventional charm similar to the versions quoted
above. How the wretched girl stood up to this excruciatingly
painful operation is not related, but certainly her arm did not.
Not unnaturally, blood poisoning set in, official medical treatment having to be sought to rectify matters and save the arm
from amputation.

The moral of this story seems to be that witchcraft, relying
solely upon thought or will-concentration, is safer and more
efficacious than when extraneous aids are introduced.

Both Baring Gould and William Crossing have published

the words of some of these healing-charms. But as with Baring
Gould's polished-up version of the original *Widecombe Fair*
song, it is evident that most of the charms have been subjected
to the same process of editing by the collectors. Compare, for
instance, the two following versions of the *Charm for Sprains*.
The first is taken from William Crossing's *Folk Rhymes of
Devon*:

> Bone to Bone and Vein to Vein,
> And vein turn to thy rest again
> And so shall thine
> In the name of the Father, Son and Holy Ghost.

Contrast this with the next quoted from the same collection of
old papers as the *Thorn Charm*.

FOR A SPRAIN

Our Lord Jesus Christ rode over a bridge. His horse lighted and
He lighted. He said, "Marrow to marrow and bone to bone and
sinews to sinews and skin to skin (and to the others). In the name
of the Father and the Son and of the Holy Ghost I cast this sprain
away. Amen. So be it.

The last sentence recalls the witches' forceful formula: "As I
will, so mote it be." Even the second version gives an impression
of the slight "tidying" of some cruder version, by the insertion
of capitals and punctuation.

There are similar types of charms for toothache, inflammation—rather a vague term—ague, and in the *Transactions of
the Devonshire Association* for 1899 are two that are very
curious and certainly very old. The first is:

FOR AGUE, FEVER OR WITCHCRAFT

When Jesus saw the Cross thare to be crucified pilate said unto
him "What aileth thee? Why shakest thou? hast thou fever, ague
or witchcraft?" Jesus said unto him "I have neither fever, ague
nor witchcraft but shake for they sins. Whosoever carryeth this
in his mind or in writing shall never have neither fever, ague or

M

witchcraft. In the name of the father and of the Son and of the holy ghost. Amen Amen."

From the reference to carrying "in mind or in writing" it appears that, if copied out, the charm might be used as an amulet to ward off the specifically mentioned evils.

The second of these charms is:

FOR BURN GOUT

Three or four fair maidens came from divers lands crying for burn-gout—acheing, smarting and all kinds of burn-gout—they went to the burrow town—there they had brethren three—they went to the salt seas and they never more returned again—he or she shall have their health again in the name of the Father, the Son and the Holy Ghost.

Whether this is a charm for the burning pains of gout, or simply for burns is a matter for conjecture, no clue being given in its contents. Once again, I should guess the original to have been unpunctuated, the dashes being inserted for clarity by some later editor, together with capitals and punctuation.

The words of these charms cannot be considered as anything but crude gibberish to which a Biblical veneer has been applied. Where then lies the power to procure results through their medium? Certainly not in the actual words. After all, words are only *sounds* used to express feelings. They have no power in themselves. Yet these old charms have been passed down through the centuries as inseparable adjuncts to the healer's success, being still treasured as such today. The only feasible explanation—if explanation it is—brings us back again to the witchcraft fundamental—concentration. These doggerels can surely serve no other purpose than to help fix the practitioner's mind firmly upon the matter in hand, much as will-force is contained within a circle.

We have already seen that the actual methods employed have no bearing upon subsequent results either, being too varied in character. The use of coins, bean pods, bacon rinds, meat, pebbles, hand-shaking or mere wishing depends upon individual fancy. It is a point of minor interest, that most of the visible agents are brought to bear upon wart-curing, other ailments being banished by intangible means alone.

The question as to *how* these results are obtained therefore remains unanswered. So also does the reason *why*. It is a remarkable fact that the great majority of natural healers belong to the humbler walks of life, many of them having had little education beyond that afforded by the old-time village school which they left at the age of eleven or twelve for a life's work in the countryside. Possibly this provides a half-clue to the mystery. Men who live nearest to nature acquire perhaps special natural gifts. These endowments seem to be accepted unquestioningly and uncritically by those possessing them, services being rendered in the same manner. Nor, as far as I know, are they ever refused, unless some grave offence or insult is offered—probably quite unwittingly—by a suppliant for help.

It is, of course, tacitly understood that no money is proffered; that act constitutes an insult in itself. Even the token payment of ½d. passes from healer to patient, not, as might be expected, the other way about. At an appropriate distance of time, say Christmas, a bottle of whisky, a tin of tobacco, or a case of beer would probably be received as an acceptable and seasonable gift. But, according to belief, if a witch takes money for his services the "power will leave him".

It is one more remarkable fact in this whole remarkable subject, not only that this "power" or "virtue" should be so highly prized and safeguarded, but that it should be at the disposal free gratis of anyone who cares to solicit help. Perfect strangers—such as the lady seeking the Sticklepath witchdoctor —are accorded the same privileges as friends and neighbours.

Three years ago, someone whom we did not even know by name, wrote from London to inquire whether we could supply her with the address of a wart-curer as she could get no relief elsewhere. For some reason the negotiations fell through before we were able to make detailed arrangements, but had she arrived her reception would have differed in no way from that accorded to any local visitor.

From which incident it may be deduced that although white witchery itself may be mainly confined to the West Country, its reputation has spread some way beyond these confines. Indeed, since this book was first published the number of letters I have received from people in all walks of life, from all parts of this country as well as from abroad craving the aid of a white witch has been really remarkable.

CHAPTER TWENTY-THREE

Adder Lore

FROM the earliest times, the serpent has been reviled and revered by mankind—often at one and the same time—in all quarters of the globe, appearing in the folklore of all lands. The feathered serpent waved its plumes on the ancient temples of the Incas. It entered the Garden of Eden to bring about the downfall of man, but later, its brazen likeness was erected by Moses in the land of Edom as a remedial measure for Israelites suffering from the bites of "fiery serpents"—another instance of sympathetic magic.

In northern mythology, it lay in the dark underworld, coiled round and perpetually gnawing at, the roots of the mighty ash-tree Ygasdril, support of the universe and counterpart of the Hebrew Tree of Life. Serpents wreathe the waist of the Indian Kali, goddess of destruction, while in Greece they writhed as the snakey locks of Medusa whose glance—possibly akin to the evil eye— also wrought destruction. In the mýstical Jewish Qabalah the serpent of wisdom raises its seven crowned heads from yet another Tree of Life. Voodoo rites are still practised in Haiti where a river-god is worshipped in the form of a serpent whose dwelling is a waterfall.

Snake-lore is indeed a fascinating and exhaustive subject, while snakes themselves are creatures that have fascinated and repelled men all down the ages. Descending from the sublime serpents of mythology, we find two insignficant representations of this lordly tribe, humbly housed in the bogs and heather of Dartmoor today. They are the harmless grass-snake and the venomous viper or adder, both of which also occur in most other parts of Great Britain.

As indentification is usually confused, both reptiles are treated with extraordinary fear and dislike by the average countryman, being battered to death without any attempt at discrimination. Neither is as common now as it was even a few years ago, for, like all wild life, the snake population is decreasing annually. The dry bracken slopes and heather banks where formerly, on any hot summer day, one heard the stealthy rustle of an adder slipping away, now conceal very few. We have always expected to come across several—dead or alive—during a season. In the last three years we have not seen a single specimen of either adder or grass snake. The latter, of course, never as numerous, are mainly confined to damp and marshy spots where, if discovered, they are dispatched with the same atavistic gusto as is a viper. The countryman evinces the same genuine deep-rooted fear of snakes as of black witches—rather more, in fact, in these days—nor does he attempt any identification before killing them in haste.

A short time ago an "expert" naturalist on a radio programme poured scorn on the generally accepted method of distinguishing between the two species. I can only say that having seen many vipers in the course of many years; having lunched a few yards from one too gorged to move though obviously resentful of our proximity, having had dogs bitten by vipers and been bitten by one myself, I find the dark "oak-leaf" or zig-zag pattern down the back, together with the inverted V-for-Viper on the back of the head, reliable identification marks. A grass snake may be recognized apart from its greater length by its double row of dorsal rings from which it is sometimes called "ringed snake"; also by the two light patches on either side of the base of its head. There should be no confusion between the two creatures.

Comparatively few years ago it was commonly believed that the first essential to recovery from an adder-bite was to ensure the death of the snake. Until this was accomplished, the patient could not recover. When cattle or dogs fall victims, the adder, of course, is seldom seen. In that case, when the animal began to show improvement, it was conveniently assumed that the reptile had met its death "somehow else".

Our moorman friend John once sought help from the Belstone white witch, leaving his dog, to all appearances dying from snake-bite, at home.

"Have you killed the adder?" was the only question the woman asked. Receiving an affirmative reply she merely said, "Very well, go home and you'll find your dog all right." He did, and was met at the door by his tail-wagging spaniel which had been left practically in a coma.

A curious superstition attached to a reptile's death is that "a snake can't die 'till the sun goes down". Its battered corpse may be left flattened out on the road, but according to local lore, it cannot be considered officially or safely dead until sunset. Most of these superstitious ideas have some basis in misunderstood or misrepresented fact. In this case it may be that the convulsive twitchings of the nervous system, which usually persist for some time after death, have given rise to this widely held belief. The discarded tails of lizard and slow-worm evince this propensity long after they have parted company with their owners. The severed tail of a slow-worm in particular continues to writhe and wriggle for anything up to half-an-hour, and to most country people the slow-worm is merely another snake, and as such asking for elimination. That it is not recognized as a legless lizard is hardly surprising considering its deceptively snake-like appearance.

Slow-worms live in our long rockery sometimes making excursions into the danger zones of neighbouring gardens. The owners are briefed as to the harmless characters of these stray visitors which are therefore afforded a grudging diplomatic immunity. One small girl, having had the difference between snake and slow-worm carefully explained, nevertheless used to creep in and be found gazing earnestly at the rock plants, hoping to be rewarded with a glimpse of "Mrs. Gordon's snake". Such it appears to be, and such it will remain I think in the minds of most people for a long time to come.

Returning to the genuinely venomous adder, two old country remedies were recommended for its bite. Should a dog fall victim out in the wilds beyond reach of witch or vet a hazel wand, if obtainable, should be twisted into a ring and placed round the animal's neck. It seems probable that this, like the shingle-healer's circle of rushes, is the magic circle in operation once more.

The second recipe is plainly a herbal "simple". Upon reaching home, fresh green ash-tips should be gathered and boiled, the resulting liquid being given to the dog as medicine. Both remedies were commonly used in this district only a few years ago.

Twice our black Labrador retriever was bitten when out with us on Dartmoor. The first time he had apparently disturbed two or three adders basking together, several places round the region of his heart having been visibly punctured. It is impossible to carry a large retriever, and as the poison began to take immediate effect it was only with the greatest difficulty that we managed to get him home. By that time a great bag of poison had formed beneath his throat, hanging like a cow's dewlap. Veterinary aid was prompt, but even so, we had to battle for his life during three days and nights.

On the second occasion we were walking on a dry bracken slope covered with gorse and hazel scrub. This time the dog was attacked on the nose which began to swell immediately. Mindful of our country lore, having twisted a slender hazel wand into a circle we popped it over his head. Thus decorated we led him home, by which time the swelling was subsiding. It was unnecessary to call the vet, and the dog continued perfectly well.

Whether this was attributable (a) to the hazel wand; (b) to the poison happening to be less virulent, or (c) to the fact that it was injected into the boney part of the nose instead of into the vulnerable region of the heart it is impossible to say. The last I should consider to be the most probable.

I have known only one dog killed by a snake-bite, and that

was a small terrier. At the time doubt was expressed whether it had succumbed to the actual poison or to some strong injections administered by the vet which seemed to bring on convulsions. During the past half century I believe only seven people are known to have died from adder-bite, very young children of course being the most vulnerable.

Had I suffered my own snake-bite say thirty years ago, on my way home I should doubtless have visited a white witch. If she had had a toad skin handy that would have been applied to the place, for toads were believed to be immune from snake-bite, probably on account of the thick, leathery texture of their skins. To accompany this act of sympathetic magic—repelling the poison by something itself considered poison repellent—there was another of these old charms:

BLESSING FOR STING
Adder, Adder, Adder, Lay under a stone or hole he hath done this beast wrong. I fold, two fold, three fold, in the Name of the Father and of the Son. So let this sting pass away from this wretched vermint if the Lord please. Amen.

This obviously very old charm from the Marystowe papers seems to make rather less sense than most. It will also be noted that the word "sting" is used, a very common but erroneous expression around Dartmoor. Adders, of course, are not equipped with stings, but with two hollow fangs. These act as reservoirs for the poison which is released when the fangs are sunk into the flesh of man or beast.

Victims of viper-bite today receive very different treatment from the old-time methods suggested above. Today the nearest telephone and car are requisitioned to summon ambulance or helicopter, which arrives on the scene probably within half an hour. The thoroughly scared patient (who may otherwise be feeling perfectly normal) is rushed to the nearest hospital and given anti-venom injections. treated for shock, and kept under observation for at least twenty-four hours. The incident receives Press headlines, and the victim becomes for a brief period a centre of interest, with anxious relatives and friends who have read their papers, or heard their local news bulletin on the radio, ringing up "to inquire".

When I read these accounts today, I compare them with my own experience, which took place soon after the last war.

After the two dog-biting episodes, on our Dartmoor expeditions we always carried a tin of permanganate of potash crystals and a small bottle of brandy in the haversack—for the retriever. On this occasion we had lunched at Knack Mine beneath Steeperton Tor, and were hunting the old heather-draped tin humps for a ring-ouzel's nest. Walking along an almost imperceptible sheep-track, winding among tall heather, I was conscious of a sudden sharp prick just above my left ankle as it brushed against the herbage. Hearing the stealthy tell-tale rustle as the invisible viper withdrew, I knew at once that no wasp or bee was to blame. Sure enough upon removing my—fortunately fairly thick—sock and shoe, there were two unmistakable blue punctures above the ankle bone. We went down to the stream—the young Taw River—where my husband sucked and spat and sucked and spat until we felt that something must have been removed. The permanganate crystals were next dissolved in a thermos cupful of cold Taw water with which the wound was bathed. Next a thick wad of sphagnum moss from the handy bog, was bound on with my husband's handkerchief. Sock and shoe were, with some difficulty, replaced, after which we decided upon a dose of brandy, only to find that the cork had popped and the bottle was empty. Tea from the thermos was substituted and there being no car, telephone, witch, hazel bush, helicopter or ambulance available, we began the long foot-trek back over the rough moor to Belstone and on to Sticklepath.

All told we had a walk of about seven miles, the course of which was punctuated by my husband's anxious inquiries as to whether I "felt all right". After our experience with the Labrador, not unnaturally he feared my imminent collapse into the heather. However by keeping steadily on, I made it, but had I not put on my shoe and started at once I should not have been able to do so. The foot was so badly swollen upon reaching home that it was almost impossible to get the shoe off, nor was I able to put my foot to the ground for several days.

The local doctor came, looked, and sent some lotion for application, but there was no mention or idea of hospital, ambulance or injection. Apart from the localized swelling I felt no ill-effects whatever. Possibly, as in the case of the retriever, this may have been due to the poison having been received in the bony structure of the ankle, rather than in some more vital or fleshy spot.

There is an old superstition to the effect that where a viper lies concealed, a dragonfly hovers above, sent by Providence to give warning of danger. The yellow and black erroneously named "horse-stinger" blunders about over the heather, while green, blue and bronze-winged demoiselles dance beside the wide marshy stream margin below Knack Mine. Yet, if one of these many ethereal beings was hovering over that particular adder on that particular afternoon, my obtuse understanding totally failed to recognize in it the quivering wings of my Dartmoor guardian angel.

When adders were rather more plentiful than they are at present, it was no unusual sight to see a dead one suspended upside down by the tail to a gate or tree branch. This practice ensured that in any post-mortem twitchings, head and tail were kept well apart. If they happened to touch, the snake would 'come alive again'. Here, once more, is evidence of belief in the continuity of the magic circle, for should the writhing extremities meet, the adder's life circle would be renewed.

So, we end as we began with that most ancient of beliefs, the all-pervading influence and mysticism of the circle. It has cropped up continuously throughout this record of Dartmoor's folklore, from prehistoric stone circles, witches' cauldrons, holy wells, magic circles to confine power whether for good or evil, dancing rings and circlets of woven rushes, down to the necklaces worn by members of today's revived witch-cult. All are manifestations emphasizing that age-old symbol of eternity.

CHAPTER TWENTY-FOUR

Postscripts

BETWEEN one edition of any book and the next, facts, opinions and situations may alter completely. What is correct today may well be out of date next week, present truths becoming tomorrow's inaccuracies. Never is this more apparent than when revising a book. Accordingly, bearing in mind both accuracy and interest, fresh data must find a place in each new edition.

For some of it, owing to technical reasons, no space can be found in the original text. In this final short chapter, therefore, material thus crowded out is presented in the form of postscripts. Each has been given its separate subject heading and chapter number for easy reference, indicated by an asterisk in the text.

White Hound of Cator (Chapter 4)

Since the first edition of this book was published, a correspondent has described a modern sighting of this hound. When walking along the edge of a plantation near Cator Gate, in full sunlight, she saw, coming towards her, a very large cream-coloured dog with long coat and ears. It came close, waving its tail in so friendly a manner that she put out her hand to pat it, exclaiming aloud: "Oh, you beautiful creature! Where have you come from?" Whereupon it vanished.

Recounting this experience later to a Widecombe acquaintance, she learned that the attractive phantom had been seen several times upon a neighbouring farm, also in the grounds of the house haunted by the black pack.

Tinners' Rabbits (Chapter 4)

In this curious device, each hare has one ear only, yet each appears to have the normal pair. Further research, however, fails to find any justification for a direct connection with alchemy. More probably, the frequent occurrences of the motif in a circumscribed neighbourhood at approximately the same dates, points, I think, to the fact that it was a favourite among itinerant wood-carvers of the period commissioned to carry out work in churches then being erected.

As a curious and unusual device, it was then probably copied by later craftsmen. It has also been suggested that the tinners, as 'burrowers' in the earth, adopted that arch-burrower, the rabbit, as a suitable emblem of their trade. However that may be, the three obvious hares became Tinners' Rabbits associated with tin wealth, possibly also having some oblique reference to the many new warrens then being established all over Dartmoor.

Lady Howard (Chapter 5)

To be historically correct, Lady Mary Howard was born in 1596, Mary Fitz, daughter of Sir John Fitz of Fitzford near Tavistock. Before the age of seventeen she had been married three times to (a) Sir Alan Percy, (b) Thomas Darcey, Earl of Essex, and (c) Sir Charles Howard, by whose name she preferred to be known although she married a fourth husband, Sir Richard Grenville, grandson of the *Revenge* Sir Richard. She was a forceful personality whose matrimonial ventures might be described as one long stormy progression. However, the popular idea that her ghostly penance was imposed as retribution for the poisoning of a selection of husbands, is untrue. Here there has arisen confusion with another Lady Howard, Lady Frances, a younger contemporary who 'did time' in the Tower of London for this offence.

The only misdemeanours really attributable to Lady Mary are the quarrels with her various husbands and indifferent neglect of her children—particularly of her daughter. But presumably this long life of family dissension has been sufficient to condemn her to an even longer period of post-mortem activity.

Lady Frances Howard, the poisoner, died in obscurity. Lady Mary Howard has inexplicably been denied even the obscurity of death.

Kit's Steps (Chapter 9)

Kit's Steps story tells us that another Kitty, a young lady, attempted to jump her horse across the gorge at this spot. The horse landed safely on the far side but without Kitty who was caught in the branches of a tree and her body left hanging there for some time before the gruesome accident was discovered.

More recently a fatality in 1968 recalled these tragedies. A young soldier returning to camp one evening, took a short cut across the Gorge. He was never seen again in spite of intensive search. Weeks later his body was found upon the surface of that dark pool aptly named the Devil's Cauldron. Bringing in a verdict of accidental death, the coroner, as reported in the press, used these words:

"He could have been overcome by the atmosphere of the Gorge which I personally think is no cheerful place even in daytime. In the gloom and damp he may have been overcome by the eeriness and had a certain compulsion to jump in . . . but there is no evidence of premeditation."

A significant echo of past voices.

Sheeps Tor (Chapter 12)

Farther away on the south-east side of Dartmoor near Meavy the long grey hump of Sheeps Tor seems to have afforded at least one of these disturbing incidents.

A naval chaplain and a friend returning at dusk along the track below the tor, were startled by blood-curdling screams close at hand among the tumbled rocks. Intense search revealed nothing unusual, but having carefully marked the spot the two men returned next day with a Dartmoor archaeologist. There he at once identified the remains of a Bronze Age settlement, including a large flat stone, possibly the capstone of a kist which, he suggested, might have been used for sacrificial purposes.

One might perhaps also suggest that the Sheeps Tor clitters afford secure harbourage for foxes. To unaccustomed ears, the squall of a vixen at night is one of the most blood-curdling of country sounds.

The Ace Fields (Chapter 13)

It has been suggested that these little intakes were originally enclosed as artificial rabbit burrows for Headland Warren during the period of Dartmoor's warrening industry.

Two of the 'Aces' have now been re-walled and ploughed, losing something of their distinctive shape in the process. The original choice of outline, however, remains unexplained.

Modern Village Charmers (Chapter 19)

The intervening years since some of the Witchcraft section was written have brought considerable changes to village life and its simplicity. As is only to be expected, the craft of the witches, charmers, healers, call them what you will, are dying out. With a few exceptions, those that remain are of the older generation and even among them there are signs of deterioration in their practising skill.

The repealing of the antiquated Witchcraft Act in 1951, sparked off a revival of interest in the cult. Modern Witch societies practising much of the old ritual have sprung into being and into inevitable publicity. Caught up also in this trend are the simple village healers. There seems no doubt that once the unsophisticated charmer has been 'discovered' by press, radio or television, the 'virtue' does indeed depart. I know several once infallible practitioners whose 'power' has thus declined with publicity.

Index